CREDIT AND BLAME

CREDIT AND BLAME

Charles Tilly

Princeton University Press

Princeton and Oxford

Library of Congress Cataloging-in-Publication Data

Tilly, Charles.
Credit and blame, Charles Tilly.
p. cm.
Includes bibliographical references and index.
ISBN 978-0-691-13578-6 (hbk. : alk. paper)   1. Attribution (Social
psychology)   2. Responsibility.   3. Blame.   4. Justice.   I. Title.
HM1076.T54 2008
302'.12—dc22   2007045225

British Library Cataloging-in-Publication Data is available

This book has been composed in Electra and American Gothic

Printed on acid-free paper. ∞

press.princeton.edu

Printed in the United States of America

1 3 5 7 9 10 8 6 4 2

CONTENTS

PREFACE

We humans spend our lives blaming, taking credit, and (often more reluctantly) giving credit to other people. Viable visions of life can include varying proportions of credit and blame, but none of us escapes the urge to assign value—positive or negative—to other people's actions, as well as our own. That is so, I speculate, because evolution has organized our brains to create accounts of actions and interactions in which X does Y to Z. X causes Y to happen, and Z bears the consequences. We don't simply observe X-Y-Z sequences dispassionately, as if we were watching how falling raindrops form a puddle on a windowsill. Instead, we assign moral weight to those sequences, deciding many times each day (usually without much reflection) whether we or someone else did the right thing. What's more, we want doing the right thing to receive rewards and doing the wrong thing to receive punishments. This book focuses on how we humans relate just rewards and punishments to other people's actions, and to our own.

Over a half century of research, writing, and teaching, most of my professional work has concerned large-scale political processes such as revolutions, social movements, and transformations of states. Anyone who has studied these sorts of processes—or, for that matter, takes part in them—sees credit and blame everywhere. Political leaders (often unjustly) take credit for their regimes' accomplishments, blame their enemies or underlings when things go wrong, and sometimes award their supporters medals, titles, and sinecures. Just as much crediting and blaming occurs in other social settings, from big corporations to modest households. At all scales, credit and blame pervade social life.

In 2006, Princeton University Press published a little book of mine. I called it simply *Why?* The book asked what happens as people give other people reasons for things they have done, things they have seen, and things other people have done. The book gave two connected answers to the question. First, reason-givers choose among four different sorts of reasons: *conventions* in the style of "Life is tough," *codes* in the style of "Those are the rules, and I followed them," *technical accounts* in the style of "Let me tell you what we doctors think causes this illness," and *stories* in the style of "Jerry got mad at Joe, and slugged him." Second, even for an identical event, reason-givers offer systematically different reasons to different receivers depending on the relationship between them; we take for granted that a psychiatrist will give a nervous mother a different sort of reason for a child's tantrums from the reasons proposed by her mother-in-law. Third, whenever people give each other reasons they are simultaneously negotiating, establishing, transforming, or confirming relations between themselves. Most reason-giving confirms existing relations, so much so that we find it surprising or threatening when someone proposes an inappropriate reason. My book *Why?* follows these insights over a wide range of social life, including reason-giving in courts of law, public debates, and efforts to make technical science accessible to non-specialists.

Credit and Blame takes up a problem *Why?* deliberately left unsolved. When we give reasons for someone's actions that significantly affect someone else's well-being, what do we do about it? To the extent that we see some connection between ourselves and the people affected by the action in question, we don't simply shrug off the effect as just one of those things, inevitable or inexplicable. Instead, we try to assign credit or blame, sometimes blaming ourselves for an unhappy outcome or taking credit for a happy outcome. More surprisingly, we seek justice in credit and blame. We don't settle for clever or comprehensive explanations of the behavior that caused the outcome in question. We ask that the punishment fit the crime, the reward recognize the accomplishment, the parties involved get just deserts. Standards of justice vary from one population and period to another. Yet justice has far more common properties than cultural relativists imagine. *Credit and Blame* identifies those common properties and shows how they work on a scale that ranges from arguments among friends to the creation of national commissions for the pacification of fierce political disputes.

Although I have been thinking about credit and blame for many years, only as I wrote this book did I realize that I had gotten one part of the analysis wrong. I had thought that credit and blame formed mirror images: blame was credit upside down. As I looked at cases, however, I began to understand that blame activates sharper distinctions between a worthy us and an unworthy them than credit does, makes that us-them boundary harder to cross than in the cases of taking or receiving credit, and almost always calls up stricter standards of correspondence between deed and response than when people share, take, or award credit. No doubt I have missed other equally important insights that will occur immediately to my readers. So much the better. Daily experience, after all, makes all of us experts on credit and blame.

Credit where credit is due. Friends who express their loyalty through sustained criticism best advance a book like this one. I am deeply grateful to Adam Ashforth, Christian Davenport, Lynn Eden, Andreas Koller, Tim Sullivan, Chris Tilly, and Viviana Zelizer for reading earlier drafts with intelligent care, and to Jodi Beder for impeccable editing.

CREDIT AND BLAME

1 | CREDIT, BLAME, AND SOCIAL LIFE

In Dostoevsky's chilling novel *Crime and Punishment*, poverty-stricken and ailing ex-student Rodion Romanovich Raskolnikov figures first as antihero, then finally as hero. At the book's very start, Raskolnikov descends the stairs from his shabby room to the St. Petersburg street. As he reflects on the crime he is contemplating, he mutters to himself:

> Hm . . . yes . . . a man holds the fate of the world in his two hands, and yet, simply because he is afraid, he just lets things drift—that is a truism . . . I wonder what men are most afraid of . . . Any new departure, and especially a *new word*—that is what they fear most of all . . . But I am talking too much. That's why I don't act, because I am always talking. Or perhaps I talk so much just because I can't act.[1]

Raskolnikov soon summons up the courage—or the frenzy—to commit a viciously violent act. With a stolen axe, he murders the aged pawnbroker Alyona Ivanovna, cuts a greasy purse from around the old woman's neck, fills his pockets with pawned objects from a chest underneath her bed, misses thousands of rubles in a nearby chest of drawers, and slaughters the old woman's long-suffering sister Lizaveta Ivanovna when Lizaveta arrives unexpectedly.

Raskolnikov then flees in panic down the stairs, almost gets caught on the way out, rushes to his miserable room, lies down feverish and exhausted, gets up to go out with his loot, hides it under a big stone in a faraway courtyard, and never retrieves his ill-gotten gains from their hiding place. Most of the novel revolves around changes in relations between Raskolnikov and other people as the imperial police close their net around him. Before the book's sentimental finale, Raskolnikov remains incapable of returning the love and admiration friends and family lavish on him despite his surly treatment of them.

With his brutal violence, Raskolnikov hopes confusedly to rise above credit and blame. Yet at his trial witnesses testify to a series of extraordinary charitable and even heroic acts Raskolnikov performed while at the university: supporting the old, ailing father of a dead classmate, rescuing children from a burning room, and more. Those deeds, his voluntary confession, and his debilitating illness win him a short prison sentence of eight years. But Raskolnikov takes no credit for charity and heroism. He identifies himself with heroes like Napoleon. They—he thinks—took their good deeds for granted. They did not hesitate to destroy for the larger good of humanity.

Later, in a Siberian prison for his crime, Raskolnikov reflects again:

> My conscience is easy. Of course, an illegal action has been committed; of course, the letter of the law has been broken and blood has been spilt; well, take my head to satisfy the letter of the law . . . and let that be all! Of course, if that were the case, many benefactors of mankind who did not inherit power but seized it for

themselves, should have been punished at their very first steps. But the first steps of those men were successfully carried out, and therefore *they were right*, while mine failed, which means I had no right to permit myself that step.[2]

Although he is paying the penalty for his crime—hard labor in Siberia—Raskolnikov still refuses to accept the blame.

In his book's closing scenes, however, Dostoevsky breaks the somber spell. The love of Sonya, the former prostitute who has accompanied Raskolnikov to Siberia, redeems the antihero and starts him toward a new life. At the very end, Dostoevsky paints in the parallel with Christ's raising Lazarus from the dead. Life, for Raskolnikov, finally entails earning credit and taking blame. Perhaps the world's Napoleons can escape the binding of human relations, Dostoevsky tells us. The rest of us, Dostoevsky implies, have no choice but to take responsibility for our actions, good or bad.

The lesson cuts both ways: social life involves taking or giving credit and blame, but assignment of credit and blame also involves relations to other people. Nihilists, saints, and utilitarians may imagine worlds in which relations to specific other humans don't matter so long as accounts come out right with the cosmos, with the gods, or with humanity at large. They are rejecting their own humanity. Raskolnikov's very effort to escape credit and blame for his actions made the point. In so doing, he was denying his obligations to specific other people, including his mother, his sister, his companion Sonya, and his faithful friend Dmitri Prokofych Razumikhin. For the rest of us ordinary mortals, however, getting relations with specific other people right matters fundamentally.

Following that principle, this book examines how people assign credit and blame for things that go right or wrong. It shows that crediting and blaming are fundamentally social acts. They are doubly social. First, people living with others do not settle for Raskolnikov's indifference to responsibility. Instead, they insist that when things go right or wrong someone caused them, and should take responsibility for the consequences. They don't settle for attributing the consequences to luck or fate.

Second, people spend great effort in assigning that responsibility to themselves and others. They complain noisily when other people deny due credit or blame. How people give credit and blame to others (or, for that matter, demand credit for themselves) depends at first on any previously existing relations between the creditor and the credited, the blamer and the blamed. But the very acts of crediting and blaming then define or redefine relations between the parties. This book shows how.

Think of your own daily life. Simply listen to other people's conversations at lunch, during coffee breaks, or on the bus. We all discuss repeatedly who deserves credit and who is to blame, especially when we don't think someone (including ourselves) has received just deserts. Even when the people involved think justice has been served, they put serious effort into allocating credit and blame: they write award citations, praise children who do well, pronounce sentences on convicted criminals, cluck their tongues over the latest scandal.

Stories about credit and blame don't simply spark the passing interest of stories about newly discovered dinosaurs, the latest movie star romance, or antique automobiles seen on the street. They call up empathy. They resonate because they raise issues in our own lives, whether or not we have any direct connection with the people involved. As we will see, in war, peace, politics, economics, and everyday social life, people care greatly about the proper assignment of credit and blame. This book asks how people actually assign credit and blame.

THE SOCIAL LIVES OF CREDIT AND BLAME

The origins of the words "credit" and "blame" clearly communicate their social basis. Credit comes from the Latin *credere*, to trust or believe. The verb's past participle *creditum* meant a thing entrusted to someone else, including a loan. No credit could exist without a relation between the persons giving and receiving credit. According to the Oxford English Dictionary (OED), still current meanings of credit include:

1. belief, credence, faith, trust
2. the attribute of being generally believed or credited
3. favorable estimation, good name, honor, reputation, repute
4. personal influence based on the confidence of others
5. honor or commendation bestowed on account of a particular action or personal quality

All except the first (which could consist simply of an individual's confidence in the earth's existence) strongly imply relations between givers and receivers of credit.

Blame comes from the Latin *blasphemare*, to revile or blaspheme. Blame only makes sense when some relation exists between the blamer and the blamed. (People do, of course, sometimes blame fate, their bad luck, evil spirits, the gods, or even themselves for their ill fortune. But even in these extreme cases they are talking about relationships between themselves and the originators of their misfortune.) Again the OED brings out the word's social basis: "the action of censuring; expression of disapprobation; imputation of demerit on account of a fault or blemish; reproof; censure; reprehension." A blames B, whether B deserves it or not.

Every act of crediting or blaming, however implicitly, invokes some standard of justice: she got (or failed to get) what she deserved. That standard applies to the object of credit or blame. If you or I assign credit or blame to someone else, furthermore, we necessarily refer to one justification or another.[3] Here we detect a difference between credit and blame: credit calls up a justification that associates giver and receiver in the same moral milieu, while blame separates two moral settings from each other. As I engage in "the action of censuring," I justify my own distinction from the culprit's world.

Persons who give or receive credit and blame care greatly about justice and its miscarriages. We observers, however, need not worry so much about whether they have acted correctly. This book does not seek general principles of right and wrong action. Here, we ask instead how people assign credit and blame, however appropriately they do so by our personal standards.

We could think of that as primarily a cognitive and emotional question: What mental and visceral stirrings lead an individual to conclude that she or someone else deserves credit or blame for something that has happened? That is how Charles Darwin set up the problem.

Darwin's third great book, *The Descent of Man*, focused on cognitive and emotional bases of morality. Darwin laid out four likely causes for the human moral sense: (1) instinctive sympathy of all higher animals for members of their own social groups, (2) memories of past actions and motives that reinforced the satisfaction from making enduring social instincts prevail over short-term desires, (3) reinforcement of the first two by language and communication with other group members, and (4) habit including "obedience to the wishes and judgment of the community."[4]

Although Darwin did not single out credit and blame directly, he did conclude that

> If any desire or instinct, leading to an action opposed to the good of others, still appears to a man, when recalled to mind, as strong as, or stronger than, his social instinct, he will feel no keen regret at having followed it; but he will be conscious that if his conduct were known to his fellows, it would meet with their disapprobation; and few are so destitute of sympathy as not to feel discomfort when this is realised.[5]

Psychologists and neuroscientists do not often use the word "instinct" these days. Now that they can simultaneously run experiments and watch the brain at work, however, they are confirming Darwin's general argument: Sociable moral principles evolved in the higher animals, and depend at least partly on relations to other group members, and on punishment proportionate to offenses.[6] To some extent, furthermore, almost all human beings prefer to behave in ways that get approval from their fellows.[7] Most of us reject Raskolnikov as our model.

In thinking about credit and blame, we therefore face an interesting choice. We could concentrate on the deep individual psychological processes, inborn or learned, that go on as people assign credit and blame. Or we could focus on how people deal with each other as they assign credit or blame. This book takes the second tack. While giving due respect to built-in moral propensities, it emphasizes a fascinating trio of related questions: What social processes produce the singling out of this individual or that as worthy of credit or blame? Having singled out someone as worthy of credit or blame, what do people do about it? How does the assignment of credit and blame affect the lives of the people involved?

All of us have enough personal experience with credit and blame to check general explanations against our own observations. My only firing from a job, for example, took place in a Chicago suburb, Elmhurst, during World War II. As a young teenager, I earned precious pocket money in a neighborhood grocery store after school and on weekends by unloading incoming shipments, stocking shelves, sweeping floors, and helping with home deliveries.

One day a bigger, stronger stock boy and I were unpacking cartons of breakfast cereal and stacking them. We (self-serving memory says "he") invented the labor-saving method of pulling cereal boxes from the carton and throwing them to each other across about six feet of distance, shouting and laughing as we tossed boxes of Wheaties and corn flakes. The store's co-owner walked into the middle of our jamboree. He fired me, but not my partner, who got off with a warning. Although the boss probably had other reasons for getting rid of me, I felt an acute sense of injustice, not to mention the blame I faced when I reported the news to my parents, who were barely scraping by on my father's uncertain income. I haven't written this book to avenge that wrong, forgotten for more than sixty years. But it illustrates the personal impact of blame.

Credit and blame operate on a much larger and weightier scale than a teenager's work history. During the 1980s, Latin American regimes that had thrown off dictatorships began establishing truth commissions that inquired into the abduction and killing of those dictatorships' enemies as well as the seizure and adoption of the enemies' children. The practice of truth commissions then generalized, most famously in the South African Truth and Reconciliation Commission presided over by Archbishop Desmond Tutu. During the twenty years beginning in 1982, more than twenty major truth commissions formed throughout the world. In 2001, a Ford Foundation backed International Center for Transitional Justice started to provide guidance for the setting up of truth commissions.[8] Box 1.1 lists the commissions established from 1982 to 2002. In all these cases, either a change of regime, a peace settlement to a civil war, or both allowed current national leaders to look back at the harm done by previous holders of power. They attempted reconciliation through confession. In the case of East Timor,

> A regulation issued on July 13, 2001 by the UN Transitional Administration in East Timor established a Commission for Reception, Truth and Reconciliation with a three part mandate: (1) to investigate human rights violations committed there between April 1974 and October 1999, resulting in the death of an estimated 200,000 East Timorese; (2) to facilitate reconciliation and integration of minor criminal offenders who submit confessions, through local "Community Reconciliation Processes"; and (3) to recommend further measures to prevent future abuses and address the needs of victims. After a months-long public nomination and selection process, seven national commissioners were sworn in on January 21, 2002 in Dilli.[9]

Such truth commissions usually devoted less effort to establishing the truth—what really happened—than to organizing

BOX 1.1
Truth Commissions, 1982–2002 (dates of establishment in parenthesis)

Bolivia (1982): National Commission of Inquiry into Disappearances

Argentina (1983): National Commission on the Disappeared

Uruguay (1985): Commission for the Investigation of the Situation of the Disappeared and Related Events, plus three other commissions, 1985–2000

Zimbabwe (1985): Commission of Inquiry, results still unpublished

Philippines (1986): Presidential Committee on Human Rights

Chad (1990): Crimes and Misappropriations Committed by Ex-President Habré, His Accomplices and/or Accessories

Chile (1991): National Commission for Truth and Reconciliation

Nepal (1991): Commission of Inquiry to Find the Disappeared Persons

El Salvador (1992): Commission on the Truth for El Salvador

Germany (1992): Study Commission for the Assessment of History and Consequences of the SED Dictatorship in Germany

Guatemala (1994): Historical Clarification Commission

Haiti (1994): National Truth and Justice Commission

Sri Lanka (1994): Commissions of Inquiry into the Involuntary Removal or Disappearance of Persons

Uganda (1994): Commission of Inquiry into Violations of Human Rights

South Africa (1995): Commission of Truth and Reconciliation

Ecuador (1996): Truth and Justice Commission

Nigeria (1999): Commission to Investigate Human Rights Abuses

Sierra Leone (1999): Truth and Reconciliation Commission

Peru (2000): Truth and Reconciliation Commission

South Korea (2000): Presidential Truth Commission on Suspicious Deaths

East Timor (2001): Commission for Reception, Truth and Reconciliation

Ghana (2001): National Reconciliation Commission

Panama (2001): Truth Commission to Investigate Human Rights Violations

Serbia and Montenegro (2002): Truth and Reconciliation Commission

Source: USIP 2005

confession and reconciliation. But they certainly worked with both blame and credit. They provided an opportunity for oppressors to confess their wrongs, something like Raskolnikov's final acceptance of his past under Sonya's influence. They also allowed new national leaders to take and give credit for earlier suffering and present magnanimity.

Not all national leaders took that path. Mozambique's President Joaquim Chissano, for example, rejected it.[10] Still, Bolivia, Argentina, Uruguay, and twenty other countries found that they could work their way toward peace by welding together credit and blame in truth commissions. If the point was to make a definitive transition to democracy, most of the commissions failed. Only a minority of the regimes listed in Box 1.1 (notably Argentina, Uruguay, Chile, Germany, South Africa, and South Korea) have so far moved securely into democratic territory. But in all cases, public airing of the dark past assigned blame to the perpetrators while giving due credit to the victims, survivors, and successors. It drew a line between worthy and unworthy citizens. It then gave repentant perpetrators a chance to cross the line into rehabilitation.

JUDGING CREDIT AND BLAME

In firing an unsatisfactory worker, setting up a truth commission, and a thousand other assignments of credit or blame, people are making surprisingly similar judgments. They are making judgments of outcome, agency, competence, and responsibility. Truth commissions and other judges identify bad things that happened, look for their agents, decide whether the agents had the competence to produce the bad outcomes, and ask further whether the agents bear the responsibility for those outcomes because they acted with knowledge of the likely consequences.

Assigning credit or blame to someone, then, means identifying that someone as the agent who caused some outcome, whether meritorious or deplorable. It means making someone an effective agent. The more serious the outcome of the agent's action, the greater the potential credit or blame. But assigning credit or blame also imputes responsibility to the agent: she didn't do it accidentally, unwittingly, or out of pure impulse. Instead she performed more or less deliberately with knowledge of the likely consequences. What's more, the agent must be competent, capable of deliberated action. We may scream at the toddler or dog that pulls a food-laden tablecloth from the table or thank our lucky stars that the toddler or dog set up a howl when a menacing stranger came through the door. But neither one gets blame or credit for a fully responsible act.[11]

Outcomes obviously vary in gravity. In the cosmic balance, a teenager's firing in the 1940s pales by comparison with the wrongs addressed by truth commissions. Think of it in terms of an act's impact on value. If an action has only a trivial impact on the value of assets and capabilities held by the people it affects, we estimate that value as close to 0. If, in contrast, whole lives are at stake, we estimate that value as high: close to 1, on a scale from 0 to 1. How much change in value the action produces measures its weight.

We must then distinguish between positive and negative changes in value: positive if an action enhances assets and capabilities, negative if the action diminishes assets and capabilities. Saving a dozen lives produces high positive value. Killing a dozen people—unless they happen to be enemy soldiers—produces high negative value. Combined with agency, competence, and responsibility, an outcome's value (positive or negative) guides the assignment of credit and blame.

Another important qualification: responsibility does not necessarily equal cause. Your judgment, my judgment, and a medical specialist's judgment as to what actually caused a given hospital patient to die often turn out to be irrelevant for the assignment of blame. Cause-effect connections usually play only a secondary and contingent part in determination of responsibility. That determination typically emphasizes judgments of intent and competence. Even legal proceedings for adjudication of responsibility normally center not on exactly what caused a given outcome, but on what the average competent person (whether doctor, lawyer, engineer, or ordinary citizen) is supposed to know and do.

A time-honored legal doctrine defines the "reasonable person" as a standard for such judgments. Here is the definition from *Black's Law Dictionary* (7th edition):

> A hypothetical person used as a legal standard, esp. to determine whether someone acted with negligence. The reasonable person acts sensibly, does things without serious delay, and takes proper but not excessive precautions—Also termed *reasonable man; prudent person; ordinarily prudent person; reasonably prudent person.*

The legal dictionary goes on to say that the reasonable person is not simply the average person but the prudent one.

It also defines reasonable care: "As a test of liability for negligence, the degree of care that a prudent and competent person engaged in the same line of business or endeavor would exercise under similar circumstances." In the case of medical malpractice, for example, testifying physicians speak mainly about the prevailing standards of practice in their field for the treatment of a given condition, not about exactly what caused the disability or death in question.[12] Judge and jury must decide whether the medical personnel accused of malpractice followed widely accepted procedures.

If an act produces no change in the status quo—no change in value—no one receives credit or blame. The more it increases value, the greater the credit, but only to the extent that the agent exercises competent responsibility. Saving a life accidentally garners less credit than saving a life deliberately, especially if the lifesaver faces serious risks by doing so.

Advice books by famous successful corporate executives typically take credit in exactly that way. Through my own deliberate efforts, they say, I added to my corporation's value. Real estate mogul and TV star Donald Trump illustrates the genre. His brash, boastful book *How to Get Rich* tells you how to emulate him. If you do so, maybe you, too, will make five billion dollars:

> More and more, I see that running a business is like being a general. Calling the shots carries a great deal of responsibility, not only for yourself, but for your troops. Your employees' lives, to a large extent, are dependent on you and your decisions. Bad strategy can end up affecting a lot of people. This is where being a leader takes on a new dimension. Every decision you make is an important one, whether there are twenty thousand people working for you or just one.[13]

To make big money, be decisive, daring, clear, and focused. Your competence will add value to the activity. Of course, it's a lot easier to take that sort of credit if you're a powerful boss, and everyone who knows otherwise remains under your thumb.

Similarly, former General Electric CEO Jack Welch boasts that his "candor" made the difference:

> From the day I joined GE to the day I was named CEO, twenty years later, my bosses cautioned me about my candor. I was labeled abrasive and consistently warned that my candor would soon get in the way of my career.
>
> Now my GE career is over, and I'm telling you that it was candor that helped make it work. So many more people got into the game, so many voices, so much energy. We gave it to one another straight, and each of us was better for it.[14]

Welch's honest appraisal of performances, he tells us, made the company hum. It added value. Jack Welch's responsibility and competence produced the positive outcome. No wonder that Barry Diller, himself one of America's most influential and best paid corporate executives, exclaims that "Jack is a life force."[15]

Blame operates in the opposite direction. The more an act decreases value, the greater the blame, but again only to the extent that the agent exercises competent responsibility for the act. In cases of corporate corruption, stockholders, courts, and the general public put plenty of energy into figuring out who knew enough to cheat, and did it. The combination of competence and deliberate promotion of what turns out to be a corporate disaster brings serious blame. Something similar happens regularly in politics. A member of the apartheid era South African Defense Forces (SADF) whose gun went off unexpectedly but lethally during a demonstration receives less blame than one who chased down an activist and shot him point-blank.

Still, we might not want to let the SADF professional off scot-free. Given the cruelty of apartheid, we might well decide that the very act of joining the regime's repressive forces deserved full blame. After all, it directly engaged the agent's responsibility and connected him or her with the immense harm those forces did to the country's African population. We would still be chaining together judgments of agency, outcome, responsibility, and competence. On the whole, victims of visible damage do not settle for "Things happen. It was the breaks." They look for someone or something to blame.

BLAME AND WITCHCRAFT

South African witchcraft provides another very different version of blame from the blame for racial segregation and oppression. By 1990, the apartheid regime that had run the country since 1948 was collapsing. After 27 years in captivity, African National Congress (ANC) leader Nelson Mandela became a free man that year. Although the National Party's F. W. de Klerk still formally held power, he was governing in close collaboration with Mandela and the ANC. Mandela would win the next presidential election, in 1994.

In 1990, Australian-American political analyst Adam Ashforth published an important book on apartheid's legal and political history. On a visit to South Africa, Ashforth then almost accidentally began a new career as a political ethnographer. From 1990 onward, he lived repeatedly with a family in Soweto (South West Township), the huge African settlement situated a few miles southwest of Johannesburg. Ashforth became part of Soweto's social life. Despite standing out as a tall Caucasian, he quickly settled into local routines. He hung out with youths on Soweto streets, drank

Castle beer with friends in shebeens, and played the violin in Zulu bands.

During a postdoctoral year in the 1980s, Ashforth had worked on his apartheid book in the research center I ran at the New School for Social Research, in New York City. We became good friends. When lectures and conferences brought me to South Africa in 1990, Ashforth invited me to stay with him in his new Soweto home. Among a number of other friends, he introduced me to a young man named Madumo. He later wrote an extraordinary book about Madumo's encounter with witchcraft.

Ambitious Madumo tried hard to get himself a university education, and persuaded Ashforth to help support his tuition and fees. (After meeting me, Madumo also tried to hit me up for school money, but somehow I evaded him.) When Ashforth returned to Soweto from New York one time in the later 1990s, however, Madumo had dropped out of sight. He no longer lived with his family, and had lost contact with almost all of his friends. Ashforth tracked him down, learning that Madumo had become a victim of witchcraft. More exactly, his younger brother and sister had accused him of witchcraft, and thrown him out of the family house. When their mother had died, other family members suspected that the uppity Madumo had fed her lethal magic herbs. Madumo knew he had not done the deed, but he came to think that someone or something had cursed him.

By the time Ashforth found him, Madumo had become convinced that he could only remove the curse by appeasing his angry ancestors. As he pulled on a cigarette, he complained to Ashforth:

"Have you ever known me like this before? No. I'm telling you, something is seriously wrong. *Seriously* wrong.

And I've tried so hard. But look what happened. Look at me! I'm an outcast. Even my family have turned their backs on me. Even my friends. Why?"

He inhaled again. "There must be a reason. There must. So that is why I'm questioning about these ancestors." He paused and looked up from where he had been studying a scorch mark in the blanket. I met his eyes but had nothing to say. "You know yourself, Adam. I never used to be thinking too much about these things of witchcraft and ancestors, even if my mother *was* spiritually inclined. But now, I have to face it. Something is wrong. Seriously wrong. I can't deny it."

"So you blame your ancestors?"

"It's not blame, exactly," he explained. "It's like they are forgetting me. Forgetting me because they think I've forgotten them."[16]

Madumo went on to say that the ancestors were refusing to protect him, no doubt because he had ignored them. When his mother was alive his brothers had gone to honor the ancestors' graves, but Madumo had dismissed those practices as expensive superstitions. Now he regretted his neglect.

Reluctantly, Ashforth concluded that he would have to help his friend conciliate the ancestors. The first phase consisted of Madumo's purification under the direction of an African healer, aided by members of an evangelical church — weeks of forced vomiting and anxious conversations with prophets. Then came three more phases: time to slaughter a chicken and hold a small feast in honor of Madumo's late mother, a wrenching, futile attempt to reconcile with the brother and sister that accused him of witchcraft, and a period of estrangement between Madumo and Ashforth.

Finally, on Ashforth's money, Madumo returned to the land of his ancestors, near the Botswana border, for his rite of expiation. That meant traveling to his ancestors' graves, organizing the sacrifice of a ram, sponsoring the brewing of beer, and staging a large ceremonial party for all who cared to attend, while Madumo himself abstained from the meat and beer. Ashforth's book chronicles the ordeal, and Madumo's recovery from the curse.

As a staunch western rationalist I long resisted Ashforth's claim that witchcraft was a compelling reality. But Ashforth eventually convinced me that in South Africa and elsewhere belief in its efficacy strongly shapes social life. In a later book, Ashforth stood back to reflect more generally on South Africa's problem with witchcraft. He saw it as threatening the country's hard-won democracy for two reasons. First, as some Africans move ahead while the great mass lose ground, the envy that feeds suspicions of witchcraft becomes more prevalent and pernicious. Second, the official denial of witchcraft means that from top to bottom the government fails to confront a problem felt acutely by ordinary South Africans in their daily lives: if the government can't check witches, how can it possibly improve life for most the population?

Ashforth ponders the situation:

No one can understand life in Africa without understanding witchcraft and the related aspects of spiritual insecurity. For those of us who derive our understanding of the world from the heritage of the European Enlightenment, however, witchcraft in the everyday life of Africa is enormously difficult to fathom. Many Africans insist that we should not even try, arguing that the outsider's interest in African witchcraft is merely a voyeuristic trifling with the exotic, a distraction from the more important issues of poverty, violence, and disease pressing upon the continent. They remind us that throughout the history of colonialism, not only were European attitudes to African spirituality derogatory, but the colonial fascination with African witchcraft served to perpetuate stereotypes of African irrationality and grounded colonial claims that Africans were incapable of governing themselves without white overlords. I might be inclined to agree with them were it not for the fact that I have seen too much of the damage that the fear of witchcraft can cause.[17]

Although Ashforth got some credit for helping rescue Madumo from witches, witchcraft in general does not much concern credit. South Africans don't boast about becoming witches. But witchcraft centers on blame. It poisons social life by infusing personal relations with the suspicion that a bad outcome occurred because someone else exercised enough agency, responsibility, and competence to cause grievous harm.

The case of witchcraft clarifies a crucial feature of credit and blame. Far beyond the assignment of credit and blame, people across the world typically package their social experiences in stories: explanatory narratives incorporating limited numbers of actors, just a few actions, and simplified cause-effect accounts in which the actors' actions produce all the significant outcomes.[18] Stories that Madumo's family and friends told about him almost ruined his life. Stories simplify. Witchcraft stories require little more than a witch, an act of witchcraft, an object of witchery, and an evil outcome. Their very simplicity increases their power.

Stories matter greatly for social life in general because of three distinctive characteristics:

1. Stories belong to the relationships at hand, and therefore vary from one relationship to another; a mother gets a different story of a broken love affair than does a casual friend.
2. They rework and simplify social processes so that the processes become available for the telling; "X did Y to Z" conveys a memorable image of what happened.
3. They include strong imputations of responsibility, and thus lend themselves to moral evaluations. This third feature makes stories enormously valuable for evaluation after the fact. It also helps account for people's changing stories of events in which they behaved less than heroically.

As compared with scientific accounts of the same events or outcomes, everyday stories radically simplify cause-effect connections. They trot out a few actors whose dispositions and actions cause everything that happens within a limited time and place. The actors sometimes include supernatural beings and mysterious forces—for example, in witchcraft, as an explanation of misfortune—but the actors' dispositions and actions explain what happened. Madumo's family packaged their accusations of witchcraft into stories about what he had done to his mother. Madumo then adopted the story of having offended his ancestors.

As a result, stories inevitably minimize or ignore the intricate webs of cause and effect that actually produce human social life.[19] Adam Ashforth lost his struggle to substitute a western rationalist story of Madumo's troubles for Madumo's family's stories and Madumo's own stories about those troubles. But stories lend themselves beautifully to judgment of the actors and to assignment of responsibility. They provide marvelous vehicles for credit and blame.

THE POLITICS OF CREDIT AND BLAME

To be sure, all stories don't simplify equally. Dostoevsky's *Crime and Punishment*, after all, overflows with stories, many of which we only start to understand as other stories about Raskolnikov and his loved ones fall into place. But the great bulk of stories we hear and tell in everyday life convey their agents, causes, and effects in radically simplified ways: someone did something to someone else, and that caused some outcome.

Although deals and compromises fill the back streets of politics, its great plazas teem with stories of credit and blame. A great deal of public politics in the United States and elsewhere consists of taking or denying credit, assigning or resisting blame. The country's very founding document, the 1776 Declaration of Independence, adroitly combined credit and blame. Speaking for the "Representatives of the United States of America in General Congress Assembled," a final statement of complaints declared:

> Nor have we been wanting in attentions to our British brethren, we have warned them from time to time of attempts by their legislature to extend an unwarrantable jurisdiction over us, we have reminded them of the circumstances of our emigration and settlement here, we have appealed to their native justice & magnanimity, and we have conjured them by the tyes of our common kindred, to disavow these usurpations, which would in-

evitably interrupt our connections & correspondence, they too have been deaf to the voice of justice and of consanguinity; we must therefore acquiesce in the necessity which denounces our separation and hold them, as we hold the rest of mankind, enemies in war, in peace friends.[20]

Here's the story: They—"our British brethren"—had the agency, responsibility, and competence to prevent the sad outcome, and therefore shared the blame with king and Parliament.

A Committee of Five drafted the Declaration: John Adams, Benjamin Franklin, Thomas Jefferson, Robert Livingston, and Roger Sherman. The five knew from the start that they had to levy strong enough charges against the British king and Parliament to justify the drastic step of repudiating British rule.[21] They took credit for American forbearance, and assigned blame primarily to the king. But they also blamed a parliament that failed to resist royal tyranny.

George Washington was away mustering the Continental Army in New York while his comrades were writing the Declaration. But as the successful rebels' first president (1789–1797), he worked both the back streets and the great plazas skillfully. As he approached the end of his second term on 18 September 1796, Washington delivered a farewell address we still read today as a model for public credit and blame. During his term, Washington had overseen the consolidation of the federal government and the securing of U.S. borders. But he had also faced the formation of political parties, the outbreak of a great European war, and a major Pennsylvania insurrection—the Whiskey Rebellion—against the government's fiscal authority. Echoes of all those events appear in the text of Washington's address to his countrymen.

Washington set a modest tone for his taking of credit:

In the discharge of this trust, I will only say, that I have, with good intentions, contributed towards the organization and administration of the government the best exertions of which a very fallible judgment was capable. Not unconscious, in the outset, of the inferiority of my qualifications, experience in my own eyes, perhaps still more in the eyes of others, has strengthened the motives to diffidence of myself; and every day the increasing weight of years admonishes me more and more, that the shade of retirement is as necessary to me as it will be welcome. Satisfied that, if any circumstances have given peculiar value to my services, they were temporary, I have the consolation to believe, that, while choice and prudence invite me to quit the political scene, patriotism does not forbid it.[22]

Thus he rebuffed any attempt to make him king or president for life. John Adams stood by, ready to take over from him.

Later in the address, Washington blamed without naming names. He warned against sectionalism, against advocates of involvement in foreign wars, against "faction":

All obstructions to the execution of the Laws, all combinations and associations, under whatever plausible character, with the real design to direct, control, counteract, or awe the regular deliberation and action of the constituted authorities, are destructive of this fundamental principle [the duty of every individual to obey the established Government], and of fatal tendency. They serve to organize faction, to give it an artificial and extraordinary force; to put, in the place of the delegated will of the nation, the will of a party, often a small but artful and enterprising minority of the community; and, according to the alternative triumphs of different parties, to make the public administration the mirror of the ill-concerted and incongruous projects of faction, rather than the organ of consistent and wholesome plans digested by common counsels, and modified by mutual interests.[23]

Despite advocating a small government with a modest military establishment, Washington called for obedience to that government's decisions, and blamed Americans who plotted against obedience.

More than two hundred years later, American politics still pivots on credit and blame. The al-Qaeda–coordinated attacks in New York and Washington, DC on September 11th, 2001 started an epidemic of credit and blame. As a New Yorker, I was not immune. At 6:50 AM the next day I sent out a message to my electronic mailing list on contentious politics. Nothing profound: my message called for students of the subject to avoid hysteria and to look systematically at causes and remedies of the sorts of terror we had just witnessed. The message closed:

Those of us who study contentious politics should resist the temptation to concentrate on ideas of repression and retaliation, which demagogues will surely broadcast. We may be able to make a small contribution to explaining how such high levels of coordination emerge among damage-doers, and therefore how to reduce threats of violence to civilians in the United States and, especially, elsewhere.

A bit of blaming appeared in the reference to "demagogues." But the message only assigned credit to my fellow New Yorkers, who had generally shown sangfroid and solidarity.

Three days later, I followed up the message with another. This one offered predictions concerning what we would eventually learn about the New York and Washington attacks. It included unconditional predictions, for example that all plotters would eventually turn out to have ties, direct or indirect, to Osama bin Laden, but not all to be directly connected, or even known, to each other. It then went on to contingent if-then predictions, which ran as follows:

- Bombing the presumed headquarters of terrorist leaders will (a) shift the balance of power within networks of activists and (b) increase incentives of unbombed activists to prove their mettle.

- If the United States, NATO, or the great powers insist that all countries choose sides (thus reconstituting a new sort of Cold War), backing that insistence with military and financial threats will increase incentives of excluded powers to align themselves with dissidents inside countries that have joined the U.S. side, and incentives of dissidents to accept aid from the excluded powers.

- Most such alliances will form further alliances with merchants handling illegally traded drugs, arms, diamonds, lumber, oil, sexual services, and rubber.

- In Russia, Uzbekistan, Lebanon, Turkey, Sudan, Nigeria, Serbia, Algeria, and a number of other religiously divided countries, outside support for dissident Muslim forces will increase, with increasing connection among Islamic oppositions across countries.

- Bombing the presumed originator(s) of Tuesday's attacks and forcing other countries to choose sides will therefore aggravate the very conditions American leaders will declare they are preventing.

- If so, democracy (defined as relatively broad and equal citizenship, binding consultation of citizens, and protection from arbitrary actions by governmental agents) will decline across the world.

Although evidence on the connections with contraband trade and Muslim dissidents remains uncertain, none of these if-then predictions turned out flatly wrong. Of course, they missed some important points. In September 2001, for example, it never occurred to me that the 9/11 attacks would help justify an American invasion of Iraq. Considering that I made them in the shadow of 9/11, nevertheless, the predictions held up surprisingly well over the following years.

Most of the electronic responses to my posting that flooded in expressed support or offered friendly amendments to my predictions. A few, however, called me a paranoid subversive. About a year later, the White House issued a declaration that made my predictions look less paranoid than they might have seemed in the immediate aftermath of 9/11.

A document called the National Security Strategy (NSS), issued by President George W. Bush on 17 September 2002, claimed broad rights for the sole remaining superpower. It took credit for the victory of freedom and equality over "destructive totalitarian visions." It blamed the "embittered few" for current threats to "our Nation, allies, and friends."[24] It described Afghanistan as "liberated," Iraq and North Korea as "rogue states" in the process of acquiring weapons of mass destruction.[25] Although President Bush had bracketed Iran with Iraq and North Korea in the "axis of evil" identified by his speech of 29 January 2002, the NSS blamed Iraq and North Korea especially for the world's terrorist threats. The NSS said that the era of state-to-state war had passed; terrorists had changed the terms of international relations. As disillusioned neoconservative Francis Fukuyama summed up:

> What was revolutionary about the NSS was its expansion of traditional notions of preemption to include what amounted to preventive war. Preemption is usually understood to be an effort to break up an imminent military attack; preventive war is a military operation designed to head off a threat that is months or years away from materializing. The Bush administration argued that in an age of nuclear-armed terrorists, the very distinction between preemption and prevention was outmoded; the restrictive definition of the former needed to be broadened. The United States would periodically find it necessary to reach inside states and create political conditions that would prevent terrorism. It thereby rejected Westphalian notions of the need to respect state sovereignty and work with existing governments, tacitly accepting both the neoconservatives' premise about the importance of regimes and the justifications for the humanitarian interventions undertaken during the 1990s.[26]

Six months before the U.S. attack on Iraq, the United States was declaring its right to prevent terrorism by outright military intervention. It blamed rogue states for their threat to peace, and claimed credit for the United States as the guarantor of world order. Like other American political centers, the White House was actively deploying credit and blame.

Fukuyama's dissent from U.S. military policy identifies an important feature of credit and blame I've only hinted at so far. When a sharp us-them boundary separates blamer and blamed, the very actions for which A blames B are often actions for which B's supporters give B credit. That occurs most obviously in the case of war, where killing that looks barbarous to one side looks heroic to the other. In the world of nationalist struggles, critics often point out that one person's terrorist is another person's freedom fighter. In the world of city administration, what one side calls urban renewal opponents often call real estate profiteering.

Us-them boundaries cut across much of politics. As a result, disputes over whether a given action deserves credit or blame figure regularly in political debate. In the case of 9/11, almost all Americans (including me) deplore the suicide bombers' taking of innocent lives. But for Osama bin Laden's supporters, it still counts as a telling blow against American imperialism. For them, it deserves credit, not blame.

CREDIT AND BLAME REVISITED

All these cases of political crediting and blaming identified relations between those who passed judgment and those who received judgment. Even my timid appeal to fellow students of contentious politics claimed a right to judge both western politicians and the enemies they were condemning. In every case, furthermore, the judges were crediting or blaming some specific agent (sometimes themselves) for a particular good or bad outcome, which meant assigning them both competence and responsibility for that outcome. They were fulfilling the relational conditions for credit and blame.

We therefore have our work here cut out for us. The work: clarifying the social processes by which people arrive at assignments of credit and blame. Let me repeat that this book concentrates on *social* processes, in which people interact with each other. Neuroscientists have been making great advances in describing, and even explaining, how individual nervous systems process cognition.[27] I try hard to avoid descriptions and explanations that contradict what scientists are learning about how the human nervous system generates recognition of right and wrong behavior, but that is not the book's subject. Instead, chapters to come concentrate on interpersonal transactions and relations, including the telling of stories about credit and blame.

The next chapter, then, goes farther than this introduction. It identifies the connections between justice, credit, and blame. It shows how people single out individuals and groups for approval or disapproval, and how they match appropriate rewards or punishments with the degree and character of their credit and blame. Chapters 3 and 4 take closer looks at credit, then at blame, considered separately. Chapter 5 closes the book by analyzing what happens when authorities (from prize committees to governments) start organizing memorials to victory, loss, and blame.

2 | JUSTICE

In 2002, Benetta Buell-Wilson was an athletic woman with a black belt in martial arts. She was also a married 46-year-old mother of two who was finishing a master's degree in education and about to start a second career as a teacher. On 19 January 2002, Mrs. Wilson was driving her 1997 Ford Explorer down a slight incline on Interstate 8 near Alpine, California.

Then, according to a vivid 2006 trial record,

Suddenly, Mrs. Wilson saw what appeared to be a metal object break loose from a motor home in front of her and bounce directly toward her windshield. As she swerved to avoid the object, the wheels on the passenger side lifted from the road, and the Explorer went out of control. The vehicle fishtailed multiple times across lanes and rolled four and half times, coming to rest on its roof on the road's shoulder . . .

As the Explorer rolled, the roof's pillars and rails crumpled, and the roof crushed down more than 10 inches, causing severe injuries to Mrs. Wilson. Inside the vehicle, she hung upside down from her seatbelt, in "crushing . . . unbelievable pain," gasping for breath and feeling as if her life were fading away. Motorists

31

stopped to assist and struggled to flip the vehicle, and rescue crews cut the roof open to remove her. An ambulance took her from the scene to a life flight helicopter, which flew her to Sharp Memorial Hospital trauma center.[1]

The crash severed Mrs. Wilson's spine. It left her paraplegic and in constant pain. In the Superior Court of San Diego County, she and her husband Barry sued the Ford Motor Company and Drew Ford, which had sold them the vehicle. During June 2004, a San Diego jury deliberated for five days. It concluded that the manufacturer acted with "oppression, fraud, or malice."[2] The jury awarded Mrs. Wilson $4.6 million in economic damages (expenses and loss of expected income) plus $109.6 million for noneconomic damages (pain, suffering, and reduced quality of life). It also awarded her husband $13 million for loss of consortium (reduction in the value of his wife's "society, comfort, and companionship").

The latter two awards greatly exceeded the amounts the Wilsons' own attorney had asked for. Superior Court judge Kevin Enright accordingly reduced the three awards to $4.6 million, $75 million, and $5 million. Ford appealed. The Court of Appeal confirmed the amounts for economic damage and loss of consortium. But it further cut the noneconomic damages to $55 million. The court concluded that the jury had acted on "prejudice or passion rather than sober judgment" and violated federal due process guidelines. That still left the total award at $64.6 million. The appeals court then sprang a standard legal device, ruling that the Wilsons could collect if they accepted the judgment, but would have to go back for a retrial if they contested the amounts. At last report, Ford was threatening to appeal—it had, after all, won thirteen previous rollover suits against the Explorer—but had not yet done so.

At the time of the preliminary 2004 judgment, Mrs. Buell-Wilson complained of Ford that "I'm the kind of driver they market these cars to and, if anything, that's the frustrating thing to me because they don't show any remorse at all." She continued that "I'd give it all back if I could walk again."[3] "Ford," she added later, "knew about [the design flaws] but they didn't fix their product or recall it. They just wanted to take money from people like me."[4] She blamed Ford for acting greedily and unjustly.

When people go to court in such cases, they may hope for large financial rewards. But they also typically play a double game of blame and credit. They seek to fix blame on the authors of their hardships, and to punish them appropriately. Yet they also seek recognition of their own merit, whether that merit consists of suffering borne bravely or of willingness to strike out at the rich and powerful. They ask for vindication. They ask for justice with regard to both blame and credit. Juries regularly respond in the same spirit.

Reviewing jury judgments of this kind, legal psychologist Neal Feigenson comments:

> If there is any overarching pattern in this complexity, it is that jurors in accident cases try to achieve what I call *total justice*. They strive to square all accounts between the parties (even though the issues the law asks them to resolve may not be framed in those terms), to consider all information they deem relevant (even if the law tries to keep them from relying on some of it), to reach a decision that is correct as a whole (even if they reach it by blurring legally distinct questions), and to feel right about their decision (even though the law discourages them from using their emotions to decide). The decisions that result are often, like common sense

itself, "right for the wrong reasons": consistent with the law, but not necessarily the result of strict adherence to legal rules and procedures.[5]

Courts won't let juries do as they please, but the drive for "total justice" leads juries to push the law as far as possible in the direction of righting relations between perpetrators and victims. To arrive at these conclusions, Feigenson analyzes transcripts of jury trials, interviews with former jurors, and experiments with mock juries.

In the Buell-Wilson case, anyway, not the jury but the courts had the last word. They rapped knuckles: the jury had made an excessive award out of "prejudice or passion." But the plaintiffs, jury, and judges agreed that Ford had acted improperly. They agreed in blaming Ford for Mrs. Wilson's terrible fate. They agreed that Ford had the agency, responsibility, and competence to bear the costs of that outcome.

Chapter 1 identified value change, agency, competence, and responsibility as components of credit and blame. But it did not get very far into how the assignment of credit and blame actually works. This chapter goes farther. It shows that people assigning credit and blame usually embed their accounts in recognizable stories that neatly bundle together agency, responsibility, competence, and outcome. It goes on to explore how justice figures in those stories, arguing that humans everywhere look for justice even if most of the time they fail to receive it or even to expect it. It then examines how the presence of sharp boundaries separating "us" from "them"—Jews vs. Muslims, blacks vs. whites, and so on—compound the assignment of credit and blame, with people on one side of a boundary taking credit for the very same actions for which people on the opposite side blame them.

DETECTING JUSTICE AND INJUSTICE

The legal system provides an echo chamber for conversations about credit and blame. It has, as we have seen, its own conversational rules. In the courtroom, both credit and blame depend on statutes, legal precedents, rules of evidence, attorneys' arguments, and jury deliberations. But, as Feigenson says, they also respond to stories that recur in everyday life. Those stories give reasons for the award of credit and blame.

A standard calculus runs through stories about credit and blame. It computes how much credit or blame actors deserve. It multiplies how much change in the value of some activity occurred, who and what caused that change, and whether some specific person(s) bore responsibility for the change. It calculates justice and injustice. Box 2.1—An All-Purpose Justice Detector—sums up the logic.

Value change, agency, competence, and responsibility multiply into an evaluation of credit or blame. Full agency, competence, and responsibility for a disaster receive a score of −1, full agency, competence, and responsibility for a triumph receive a +1. All real cases fall somewhere between −1 and +1. If I take the blame for a disaster, I deplore my agency, (in)competence, and (ir)responsibility. If I give you credit for a positive outcome, I stress your agency, competence, and responsibility.

The justice detector comes with a bonus. You can easily turn it into a phony justice detector. If you accept the detector's principles, you can evaluate someone else's claims of credit and blame. All you need do is make your own evaluation of the elements. Identify the relevant activity, single out the crucial actor, pinpoint the action(s) in question, specify the effect, figure the actor's contribution to that effect, estimate the value change, rate the actor's competence and

BOX 2.1

An All-Purpose Justice Detector

ANSWER THESE QUESTIONS

1. *Activity*: What valued activity do you have in mind: an organization's operation, an artistic creation, a life, human welfare in general, or something else?
2. *Actor*: Whose impact on the activity are you judging? Call them Agent X.
3. *Action*: What action by Agent X are you looking at?
4. *Effect*: What's the effect of that action on the activity you're judging?
5. *Agency*: How much did Agent X's actions contribute to the effect? Rate from 0 (no contribution) to 1 (the whole thing).
6. *Value Change*: How much did that effect increase or decrease the activity's value? Rate from −1 (wrecked it) to +1 (made it perfect).
7. *Competence*: To what extent did X have the knowledge and skill to anticipate that effect? Rate from 0 (utterly incompetent) to 1 (entirely competent).
8. *Responsibility*: To what extent did X intend that effect? Rate from 0 (completely unintentional) to 1 (planned every detail).

COMPUTE CREDIT OR BLAME

Multiply the scores for Agency, Value Change, Competence, and Responsibility, which yields a total score from −1 (X takes on huge blame) to 0 (X takes neither credit nor blame) to +1 (X gets all the credit).

If you're looking at multiple actions by Agent X, calculate the impact of each action on the activity separately, then average over all the actions.

To compare credit or blame for actions affecting different activities, weight total scores for the relative values of the activities, for example by rating an individual's life or death as a thousand times weightier than the same individual's self-esteem.

responsibility, multiply the elements, and voilà: your own assignment of credit or blame. Thus you can second-guess Donald Trump when he tells you that his leadership produced a five-billion-dollar gain in his corporation's value. Or you can reevaluate the San Diego jury's imputation of blame to the Ford Motor Company.

Once you have built your own justice detector for the case at hand, you may well want to fit it with special devices. You might, for example, want to sum Agent X's actions over a number of different events in order to detect X's long-term impact on the valued activity. Or you might want to weight values of different activities relative to each other, for instance assigning much greater weight to saving a life than to bolstering someone's self-esteem. You would still be estimating value change, agency, competence, and responsibility.

In the Buell-Wilson case, the Wilsons' lawyers didn't have much trouble establishing value change; the crash ruined Mrs. Wilson's previously full life. But they had their work cut out for them when it came to establishing agency (did the Ford Motor Company do, or fail to do, something that contributed to the crash?), competence (should Ford have known about the likely outcome?), and responsibility (did Ford actually intend to build the car it built?). The lawyers called in technical experts to testify on the Ford Motor Company's agency, competence, and responsibility for Mrs. Wilson's injuries:

> The Wilsons submitted evidence at trial that the accident and resulting injuries were caused by two independent defects in the 1997 Explorer. They established that the Explorer's design was dangerously unstable and prone to rollover due to its overly narrow track width and high center of gravity. They also established

that the Explorer's roof was inadequately supported and defectively weak, so that it readily crushed into the passenger compartment when subjected to the forces inherent in a foreseeable rollover.[6]

But the lawyers also told more general stories about value change, agency, competence, and responsibility. The *San Diego Union-Tribune*'s news report on the trial, for example, quoted Jerome Falk, the Wilsons' appeals lawyer. Falk simplified the judgment for public consumption:

> Moreover, he said the court's rejection of a new trial bid was significant, too. He noted that the justices said Enright did not abuse his authority when he barred certain evidence, and there was "plenty of evidence to support the very harsh view of Ford (at the trial) and their willingness to market dangerous products."[7]

Falk's retelling of the trial outcome recasts it as a moral tale, rightly fixing blame on the Ford Motor Company. But it activates a justice detector. Both in courtrooms and in everyday life, assignment of credit and blame consists mainly of locating agency, outcome, responsibility, and competence within simplified cause-effect narratives.

In jury trials for accidents, Feigenson points out, the narratives often take the stylized form of melodramas in which

a. events, such as accidents, are caused by individual human agency;

b. the acts of individuals are explicable in terms of their characters;

c. the agents involved in the accident can be divided into "good guys" and "bad guys";

    d. the focus of the narrative is the accident victim
       and his or her suffering; and

    e. the good guy wins (at trial) and the bad guy gets
       his or her comeuppance.[8]

Melodramas build on beautifully simplified but recognizable stories, well suited to convincing a jury of credit and blame. Melodramas supply values for the jury's justice detector.

Stories do plenty of heavy lifting in everyday social life. For everyday purposes, they have great advantages over legal interpretations and scientific accounts: they neatly adapt to the relationships at hand. They rework and simplify social processes so that the processes become available for the telling. They include strong imputations of responsibility, thus lending themselves to moral evaluations. As you can tell from your own conversations or from judicious eavesdropping in cafés or trains, people spend plenty of time making moral judgments of themselves and others. They regularly use stories to package those judgments.

Porter Abbott's fine introduction to narrative tells us how stories work. Abbott argues that narrative is "the principal way in which our species organizes its understanding of time."[9] He makes a suggestion that looks plausible to me: that evolution has wired language-based narrative into human brains. Within time, humans use ordinary language to place sequences of causes and effects. As it happens, Abbott himself[10] distinguishes between a story ("the event or sequence of events") and narrative discourse ("how the story is conveyed"), but for our purposes the simpler term "story" will do the job.

As Abbott concedes:

Most speakers of English grow up using *story* to mean what we are referring to here as *narrative*. When in casual conversation, English speakers say they've heard a "good story," they usually aren't thinking of the story as separate from the telling of it. When a child wants you to read her favorite story, she often means by that every word on every page. Leave a word out and you are not reading the whole story. But as I hope will become clear as we go on, the distinction between story and narrative discourse is vital for an understanding of how narrative works.[11]

Yes, but. When a journalist, novelist, lawyer, or sociologist writes a story, she chains together observed or imagined events into a cause-effect sequence involving some sort of agency. Let's avoid complexity by referring to that act of analysis and representation as a story.

Whatever we call it, most of the time people all over the world organize the assignment of credit and blame in simplified cause-effect sequences involving well-defined agents and outcomes. They ignore many complications. They tell stories. That simplification greatly eases the identification of agency, competence, responsibility, and outcome. If the agent was competent, if the agent's awareness of his action's likely consequences made him responsible, and if the action produced a substantial increase in value, we give the agent credit. If the action produced a substantial decrease in value, we blame him.

Rewards and punishments follow. In general, the greater the estimated increase in value, the larger the reward to the person receiving credit; saving a king's life, alas, trumps saving a serf's life. Similarly, the greater the estimated decrease in value, the larger the punishment to the person receiving blame; at least on a first offense, murder gets you a longer prison term than simple assault. Although the calculus of value change becomes much more difficult in the worlds of science and literature, the logic of awards runs along pretty much the same track: the wider the recognized impact of a discovery or a new creation, the larger the reward. Compiling judgments of agency, competence, responsibility, outcome, and appropriate reward or punishment, we produce a story of credit and blame.

Even if the basic story structure results from wiring in the human brain, the *contents* of stories vary with their cultural settings. Which characters, which actions, which outcomes, and which links among them strike listeners as recognizable and credible depends on their previous experience within the culture. The culture supplies a cast of plausible agents, and rules out other implausible agents. Witches, for instance, no longer figure as plausible agents for evils in American culture, but they do in South African culture. In both cultures, however, corporations become plausible agents, and therefore possible objects of either credit or blame.

The Buell-Wilson jury concluded that the Ford Motor Company acted with "oppression, fraud, or malice" and thus caused the structural defects in its Explorer. That conclusion drew on jury members' familiarity with American automobile manufacturers and with previous stories about SUV rollovers. It also reflected coaching by the plaintiff's attorneys and their expert witnesses. The jury apparently compressed their knowledge into a fairly simple story: Ford produces cars with high-risk defects. As a result, Mrs. Wilson's ordinary maneuver on a California highway turned into a life-shattering crash. The rendering of total justice, as described by Neal Feigenson, conforms perfectly to storytelling logic. Like a classic drama, it "squares the accounts" among all the story's actors.

Yet we pay a price for using stories. Studies of television news' impact clearly show the difference between reporting single episodes in story form and offering in-depth thematic treatments of the same subjects. When news reports focus on episodes that dramatize a poor person's plight, viewers look for someone (the poor person or someone else) who caused the hardship. When news reports take up poverty more generally, using individuals to illustrate the general theme, viewers more often attribute responsibility to government and society at large.[12] When doing total justice, we have a choice between singling out one or two culprits or tracing the whole complicated process that brought someone grief.

DOING JUSTICE

Either way, the theme of total justice recurs in big-ticket jury awards. In January 2005, a Bergen County, New Jersey jury awarded $135 million in compensatory and punitive damages to seven-year-old Antonia Verni of Cliffside Park and her mother Fazila. Attorney David Mazie hailed the verdict:

> Today Antonia Verni finally got the justice she deserved. Hopefully, the jury's decision will make a difference in the alcohol service at stadiums across the country.[13]

Before, during, and after a New York Giants football game on 24 October 1999, carpenter Daniel Lanzaro had bought and drunk almost six quarts of beer. After post-game visits at two go-go bars, he had driven his truck into the Verni family's car as they returned from a pumpkin-picking trip. Antonia's father Ronald Verni was driving a rented Toyota, with his wife and Antonia, then two years old, in the back seat. Antonia, who had vomited on her car seat earlier that day, was wearing a standard adult seat belt. Antonia emerged from the crash a quadriplegic, while her mother sustained substantial injuries. Lanzaro received a five-year prison term for vehicular assault.

The Vernis sued Lanzaro, the Giants, the National Football League, the New Jersey Sports and Exposition Authority, the rental car agency, Toyota, and the Aramark Corporation, the concessionaire whose vendors sold Lanzaro his beer at the stadium. All but Aramark settled with the Verni family, for a total of about $1.9 million. But Aramark (or rather the web of corporations that actually sold liquor in the stadium) insisted on going to trial. They lost the trial, but appealed successfully for a new trial on the basis of procedural errors in the Bergen County judgment.[14]

Aramark's attorneys had argued that the Vernis' use of an adult seat belt for a two-year-old implicated Ronald Verni in the blame for Antonia's quadriplegia. They lost on that point. The main legal dispute, in any case, had little to do with the immediate causes of the mother's and daughter's injuries. It centered on whether Aramark vendors had sold alcohol to a "visibly inebriated" Lanzaro, and thereby violated the law. In the appeal court's judgment, attorney Mazie, his many witnesses, and the Hackensack trial judge had failed to establish exactly who bore the legal responsibility for selling an already drunken Lanzaro his beer at Giants Stadium. The appeals court ruled that Mazie's evidence of a "culture of intoxication" at Giants Stadium was likely to mislead the jury.[15] It seems likely, however, that the Verni family will eventually collect a substantial share of the original award.

If you have suffered an accident, do not take these huge awards as your inspiration for going to court. According to a U.S. Justice Department report for 2001 on tort trials in the country's 25 largest counties:

- Only 3 percent of tort cases went to trial, while 73 percent ended in settlement before trial.

- About half the trials resulted from automobile accidents.

- Juries decided 93 percent of all cases that actually went to trial, but plaintiffs won only 52 percent of those cases.

- Between 1992 and 2001, the median damage award declined from $64,000 to $28,000.

- Only 5 percent of successful plaintiffs received punitive damages like those awarded to the Wilsons and the Vernis, and their median value was $25,000.[16]

Since lawyers' fees take a significant share of settlements in successful cases, Americans don't get rich by suing for accidents.

Yet they do look for justice, often total justice. Feigenson describes the case of *Giulietti v. Providence & Worcester Company*, a Connecticut federal case from 1981. Twenty-year-old John Giulietti was running a three-man crew that was trying to hook up railroad cars at night. The rear of the car he was riding backed over an incorrectly aligned switch, smashing the car into a line of cars on another track and crushing Giulietti to death. Giulietti's family sued the Providence & Worcester Railroad.

The applicable law demanded a lot: the plaintiff (Giulietti's estate) had to prove both that the railroad neglected its obligations and that the railroad's neglect caused the death. Even in that case, furthermore, the law allowed a reduction in the penalty proportionate to the worker's (Giulietti's) own negligence. In these legal circumstances, Giulietti's lawyer tried to maximize the railroad's negligence and minimize Giulietti's negligence. The railroad's lawyer, of course, tried to do the opposite: put the spotlight on Giulietti's fault.

The railroad lawyer portrayed Giulietti as totally responsible for the fatal accident. Giulietti's lawyer faithfully made the case for the railroad's negligence. But notice how he summed up:

> The family does not want any sympathy. They have re-
> ceived buckets and buckets of sympathy. Today being
> Johnny's twenty-first birthday, they have received more
> sympathy than anyone could imagine. What they are
> here today in court for is to vindicate Johnny. In order
> to vindicate Johnny, I think you would be proud to re-
> turn a verdict between one and a half and two million
> dollars. I think if you return a verdict in that range, that
> you would be proud to look anyone in the eye and tell
> them that you gave a full cup of justice to the Plaintiff
> in this action.[17]

The jury didn't quite go all the way. They awarded Giuliet-ti's survivors about $500,000, diminished by 1 percent for Giulietti's contributory negligence.[18] They were doing justice as they saw it. They were allocating credit and blame.

Feigenson argues that juries usually try to render not only justice, but *total justice*. They do so in five related ways:

1. balancing the accounts among litigants
2. using all the available information
3. reasoning holistically rather than following the separate procedural steps the law entails
4. feeling right about the decision
5. within the jury itself, following fair procedures and therefore increasing their own self-esteem.[19]

In short, far from turning themselves into legal computers, jurors bring their common sense of justice into the jury room.

The drive for total justice applies much more generally. Lawyer and legal philosopher Lawrence Friedman describes a three-stage historical process in the United States. First, life in general grew much more complicated from the nineteenth century onward. Second, both government and law expanded to meet the challenges of a more complicated world. Third, legal culture changed: Americans developed a general expectation of justice and of recompense for injustice. Friedman puts it this way:

> Justice is not only fair treatment by other people and by government; it also means getting a fair shake out of life. Life is certainly "unfair" if a man buys a can of soup and dies of food poisoning. If a person is hurt in a tornado, or hit by a car, or born with some terrible defect, these situations, too, can be described as unfair. People even *call* them unfair, even though they know that nobody is really "responsible." They also tend to feel that there ought to be some sort of redress; someone should pay.[20]

Friedman's scheme helps explain the explosion of law, lawyers, and litigation in the United States over the last century.

Yet it misleads us in one crucial way: it fails to distinguish between the demand for justice and the *expectation* of justice. Well outside the United States and since well before the twentieth century people have usually evaluated what happens to them and other people in terms of justice. They have allocated credit and blame on the basis of those evaluations. But most of the time they have recognized a brute fact: there was little they could do either about credit and blame undeserved or about credit and blame deserved but not received. Undemocratic, tyrannical regimes left little room for justice except on a very local scale. The growth of relatively democratic regimes with fairly extensive and stable legal systems did not build up the demand for justice so much as the expectation that ordinary people could get their share of it. Democracy makes it easier to expect justice.

Over most of history, people have demanded justice, but haven't received it. Even today, over much of the world public justice runs as short as clean water, good jobs, and adequate medical care. One sign of the shortage is the frequency with which poor and powerless people take the law into their own hands when they dare.[21] They often use what James Scott, a veteran observer of Malaysian peasant villages, calls "weapons of the weak": sabotage, organized foot-dragging, and clandestine attacks on exploiters' property.[22] It's not just Malaysia. Although some of the violence that prevailed in America's Wild West before farmers, ranchers, and miners settled down flowed from vicious competition and outright crime, a large share of it involved rough justice by local citizens.[23]

The scope of rough justice shrank enormously in the twentieth-century United States. Courts, police, and local authorities took over a great deal of justice-giving. That didn't happen in most poor countries. A World Bank study of very poor people's lives across the world reported how villagers in Malawi had made themselves a bit less weak by taking the law into their own hands:

> People in Mtamba and Chitambi say that not only are the police unhelpful, but "Normally, they send us back to catch the murderers and thieves and bring them to the police station. Who dares to try to catch a robber armed with an AK47 rifle?" Yet in some urban and rural areas mob justice has become a common alternative to police procedures. A discussion group in Mtamba explains, "Now the people are just punishing

the thieves on their own. They burn them. For example, last week two thieves were beaten to death because the police do not punish them accordingly." Similarly, in Mdwadzulu, a participant reports that "when a thief is caught, he is sometimes beaten up by children or even stripped naked." Thieves may be stoned, beaten, or burned to death. In Phwetekere and Mdwadzulu, participants say they sometimes take the law into their own hands out of frustration at seeing thieves released from police stations a day after being caught. "Just last week a thief was burnt to death," note discussion group participants in Phwetekere. Less extreme measures in Phwetekere include a neighborhood watch started by residents who have banded together to help discourage crime in the community.[24]

During the fierce resistance of South African townships like Soweto to apartheid during the 1980s, activists often punished suspected informers and witches by filling an automobile tire with kerosene or gasoline, hanging the tire around the person's neck, and setting the fluid on fire; they called the punishment "necklacing."[25] Once apartheid ended and something like the rule of law emerged, that grisly form of community justice disappeared. With the development of democratic institutions, regular policing, and more or less reliable courts, self-administered justice becomes less common above the scale of household or neighborhood.[26] Credit and blame do not lose importance, but they more often become grist for governmental mills.

GAUGING JUSTICE

Even in richer and less troubled countries than Malawi and South Africa, however, ordinary people worry about justice.

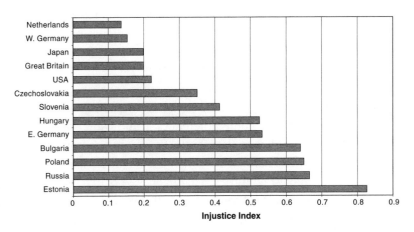

Figure 2.1. How unjust is your income (1991–1992)? (Source: Jasso 1990, Table 6)

Take a simple question: How does your actual income compare with the income you deserve? The question directly involves credit, because it asks whether whoever or whatever determines your income gives you enough credit for your contribution. It involves blame a bit less directly, but still it asks who caused whatever deprivation you suffer.

You might think that the answer is simple: everyone thinks she gets less than she deserves, perhaps half a proper income. But the comparison varies across individuals and countries. Sociologist Guillermina Jasso has done a fascinating, complex comparison of thirteen countries in 1991–1992, using responses from a large international survey. Among other things, respondents reported both their actual income and what they would consider their just income. Jasso then constructed indexes comparing the two. Figure 2.1 graphs a simplified version of one index.

In every country, on the average, people thought they received less income than they deserved. That comes as no surprise: so do I. But the differences varied systematically by type of country. It wasn't just a matter of national income: the average American reported more injustice than the average person from the Netherlands, West Germany, Japan, or Great Britain, all of which had average incomes in the same high range as the United States. The greater inequality and visibility of income differences in the United States probably contributed to that result. People in post-socialist countries, however, reported much greater injustice than people in capitalist countries. That happened partly, I think, because they compared themselves with people in capitalist countries. With the exception of Estonia, the more industrial and westernized post-socialist countries reported less injustice than the rest.

Estonians complained more than most post-socialist people. They probably complained more because their close neighbors in Finland and Scandinavia resembled them so much, but were living so much more comfortably. After all, during the decades of Soviet rule many Estonians resented the presence in Estonia of a better-off Soviet-backed Russian minority, the Estonian and Finnish languages come close to being mutually comprehensible, and with only fifty miles of crow's flight distance between Tallinn and Helsinki, cosmopolitan Estonians had been watching Finnish TV long before the Soviet Union collapsed.[27] Conclusion: of course people all over generally want more income, and compare themselves enviously with others they regard as no more deserving who get more than they do. But when judging the justice of their incomes, they also take seriously the security and other benefits the current regime gives them.[28] According to Jasso's comparisons, the Dutch saw themselves as getting more economic justice than Americans thought they received.

All sorts of humans long for justice. But they act on that longing variably depending on the social conditions in which they live. An enterprising group of social scientists has recently added to the evidence for that claim. Elementary economic doctrine assumes that people act individually and selfishly; they maximize individual advantage over a wide range of circumstances. "However," remark the authors Joseph Henrich and his collaborators,

> experimental economists and others have uncovered large and consistent deviations from the predictions of the textbook representation of *homo economicus*. Literally hundreds of experiments in dozens of countries using a variety of experimental protocols suggest that, in addition to their own material payoffs, people have social preferences: subjects care about fairness and reciprocity, are willing to change the distribution of material outcomes among others at a personal cost to themselves, and reward those who act in a pro-social manner while punishing those who do not, even when these actions are costly.[29]

Those "literally hundreds of experiments" had two serious drawbacks. First, they took place almost exclusively in college classrooms. Second, they did not assemble systematic information about the impact of the cultural, economic, and political context on the way people behave in such experiments.

An ambitious comparative study repaired these defects. The investigators went to fifteen small, distinctive, and relatively isolated populations in Africa, Central Asia, South America, and New Guinea. In each one, they studied the context of economic behavior and ran variants of four classic experiments:

> *The Ultimatum Game.* Player A receives a sum of money, and offers some part of it to Player B. B either accepts or rejects the offer: (a) if B accepts, A and B take away their agreed-upon shares, but (b) if B rejects the offer, neither A nor B gets anything.
>
> *The Dictator Game.* Just like the Ultimatum Game, except that B has no choice to accept or reject the offer.
>
> *The Voluntary Contributions Game.* Each player receives some money at the outset; each has the opportunity to make an anonymous contribution to a group fund, and the experimenters then augment the group fund by 50 or 100 percent before distributing it equally to all players.
>
> *The Common-Pool Resources Game.* Each player can make limited withdrawals from the group fund, and after withdrawals the experimenters augment the fund and distribute it equally.[30]

In the Ultimatum Game, we might expect a self-interested A to guess at the minimum offer B would accept, in hope of taking away the rest. An altruistic player, however, could offer the partner a larger share, even a fifty-fifty split. In all the games, players face stark choices between egoism and altruism.[31]

To an impressive extent, players choose altruism. In all populations, players chose to help other players far more than simple self-interest would dictate. That meant both making larger initial offers, and making larger contributions to the common fund. Second players also regularly rejected miserly offers, preferring nothing to an unfairly small share. In the

Ultimatum Game, for example, an even split between A and B came in first or second among all offers in eleven of the thirteen populations. Yet populations varied significantly in both initial offers and rates of rejection.

Statistical analyses of the results show that the extent of a population's integration into markets and (especially) general public payoffs to cooperation within the population promoted higher levels of altruism. (Some of the hunting and gathering populations, for example, punished individuals who refused to share their catches when they returned from hunting; those populations qualified as giving payoffs to cooperation.) Individual-level characteristics, in contrast, had little systematic effect on players' strategies.[32]

Exactly what produced the culture-to-culture variation remains debatable. Does market integration, for example, give people more experience with settings in which people actually do use money to benefit others, or does it expose people more to western norms of fair play in games? Probably some of each. But the findings have clear implications for the study of credit and blame. Over a wide range of populations, and perhaps over humanity as a whole, people care not merely about self-interest but also about justice. When they have a chance to act accordingly, they generally try to reinforce fairness, reciprocity, and cooperation. Evolution might have selected for humans who cooperate with each other.[33] They give each other credit for cooperative behavior, and blame each other for behavior they see as uncooperative.

US vs. THEM

Henrich and collaborators did not investigate a crucial question for credit and blame: what happens when a sharp boundary separates people who assign credit or blame from the objects of their judgments? Giving credit happens most often within boundaries. It's easier to attribute agency, competence, and responsibility for good deeds to people on our side, yet crediting sometimes crosses boundaries. Embattled countries set up peace and reconciliation commissions with the hope that malefactors' contrition will foster mutual comprehension, and even credit for willingness to confess. We often blame people close to us for this dereliction or that; just listen to children complain about how a sibling took a favorite toy or gave them a kick. But blaming occurs even more easily across boundaries such as Hindu-Muslim or black-white. On the average, us-them boundaries add a presumption of blameworthiness to everyday interactions.

Us-them boundaries also promote a peculiar sort of symmetry in credit and blame. As the case of war shows most clearly, the very acts that receive blame from one side receive credit from the other side. During the brief war of July–August 2006 between Israel and Hizbollah in Lebanon, supporters of Israel treated Hizbollah's capture of Israeli soldiers and subsequent rocket attacks on Israel as unforgivable barbarities. Meanwhile, Hizbollah supporters cheered the same deeds as heroic blows against an oppressor. On the other side, Israeli aerial bombardments of suspected Hizbollah sites within Lebanon temporarily united fractious Israelis behind their government. The same bombardments called out condemnation for their barbarism not only from Hizbollah but from opponents of Israel across the world.

As a ceasefire came into effect, Hizbollah leader Sayyed Hassan Nasrallah declared victory: "We are before a strategic and historic victory, without any exaggeration," Nasrallah said. "We emerged from the battle with our heads high, and our enemy is the one who is defeated."[34] About the same time, Israeli Prime Minister Ehud Olmert said that the ceasefire agreement would ensure that "Hezbollah won't continue to exist as a state within a state."[35] Credit and blame attached simultaneously to the same actions.

The peculiar symmetry shows up in less lethal conflicts than interstate war. Under the telling title *Stories of Difference and Equality*, Alejandro Grimson analyzes different sorts of encounters between Bolivian immigrants and porteños — inhabitants of the Buenos Aires port city and region. Most Bolivian migrants have come from the Andes. On the average, they do better economically in Argentina than in Bolivia. Yet they stand out from native Argentines, on the average, by their smaller statures, darker skins, and native speaking of Quechua, Aymara, or other Andean languages. In Buenos Aires, furthermore, they mostly occupy the classic subordinate positions of low-wage immigrants: day labor, garment work, domestic service, and similar occupations. Porteños often refer to them by the demeaning labels "bolito" and "bolita."

Grimson studies three main arenas of encounter between bolivianos and porteños: a variety of public places (public transport, street corners, and workplaces); Bolivian fiestas in the city; and mass media. In each setting, Grimson finds the immigrants facing stigma, but countering it with claims of equality or even superiority. A Bolivian named Ana describes her bus ride:

> When you ride the bus, you make sure to hang onto something so you won't fall. When I hold on, I see that women grab their pocketbooks as if someone was going to rob them. I'm supposed to move, move away so they won't think so. But I move closer and squeeze my pocketbook. I have fun. These are games I play. But now I'm not playing. If they clutch their pocketbooks, I clutch mine even tighter, as if they were going to rob me.[36]

Although some Bolivians disguise themselves as Argentines from the Andes, over and over Grimson hears from immigrants about the strategies they use to fend off threats from predatory police, exploitative employers, and disdainful porteños.

One of the most impressive conversions of blame into credit occurs in Bolivian media and festivals, with their claim to represent the authentic, ancient American culture as compared with the "immigrant" culture of Buenos Aires. The port region did, after all, receive huge waves of European immigration from the 1870s onward.[37] Each October Bolivian immigrants of the Charrúa barrio stage the Fiesta of Our Lady of Copacabana, which attracts many native Argentines to its displays of Bolivian dance, crafts, costume, and cuisine. The gala festival gives *bolivianos* a vital, visually attractive setting in which to assert their distinctiveness, and even their superiority.

An announcement of the 1996 fiesta in the local paper included these words:

> We Bolivians are landholders, while you Argentines—
> especially you porteños—are not landholders, but emi-
> grants who came to occupy a territory. You are all
> descendants of foreigners; your ethnic group and your
> ancestors were European. Instead we own our own land,
> the land called Bolivia, as descendants of Aymaras and
> Quechuas. It is therefore important that we preserve our
> identity, since we own a specific territory, since our an-
> cestors tilled that soil and the land is ours. People from
> Jujuy own their own land because the Incas formerly
> extended all the way to Tucumán. For these reasons
> it is important for us to maintain our identity because
> we are lords of that land, we are lords of all South

America, we are the natives, we are not from Europe, we are not immigrants.[38]

Argentina's Jujuy province abuts the Argentine-Bolivian border, and the city of Tucumán dominates an Argentine province almost 400 miles south of the border. As descendants of the Incas, in such a statement Bolivians are laying claim to a substantial chunk of today's Argentine territory.

Here we witness a bold reversal of subordination, a striking substitution of credit for blame. Seeking justice in the face of discrimination, Bolivians claim superior virtue. These assertions of superiority, to be sure, fail miserably to overturn the overall subordination of Bolivian immigrants in the Buenos Aires metropolitan area. But they neatly illustrate the effects of a sharp us-them boundary on the attribution of credit and blame. Us-them boundaries introduce a peculiar symmetry.

As a result of us-them boundaries, credit and blame operate asymmetrically. Everyone within a given population can agree on blaming an outsider, someone on the opposite side of the boundary. Sometimes it happens almost automatically: all those Muslims (Christians, Jews, Hindus, Irish, blacks, communists, Democrats, — name your category!) are bad by definition. Agreeing on credit for one insider, however, always diminishes possible credit for at least one other insider.

Every time someone receives a Nobel Prize in some field, for example, knowledgeable insiders discuss who else might have received, or at least shared, credit for the same or equivalent accomplishments. James English remarks that

The Nobel Prize in Literature set off a judging scandal in its very first year, when the Swedish Academy failed to name Leo Tolstoy its laureate, presenting the prize instead to the minor French poet Sully Prudhomme. And then, amid the consequent storm of protest, the academy was loath to appear contrite (or vulnerable to the pressure of public opinion) and so persisted in neglecting the Russian until his death in 1910. The scandal of appalling omissions from the roster of Nobel laureates (Tolstoy, Hardy, Ibsen, Kafka, Proust, Valéry, Rilke, Joyce, and others), so often invoked against the prize by present-day observers, was thus already firmly lodged in the field of discussion by 1902.[39]

Almost every award of a visible prize, down to levels far less prestigious than a Nobel, triggers a similar hue and cry. Within the academic world I have inhabited for many years, people prize prizes for themselves and for people connected with them. If they live close enough to the seats of power, they work to influence awards of prizes, citations, and honorary degrees. They look for recipients who will visibly exemplify the achievements they regard as worthy of emulation. They seek recognition for their sorts of people and, at a distance, for themselves.

Why, then, all the controversy? The reasons aren't obscure: the "insiders" I lumped together earlier actually fall into cliques, factions, and patron-client networks.[40] Credit given to one clique, faction, or patron-client network detracts from the standing of its competitors. As a result, the awarding of credit often becomes more contentious than the assignment of blame. Santiago Ramón y Cajal, winner of the Nobel in medicine for 1906, complained that

A few histologists and naturalists who always distinguished me with their disdain or their unfriendliness rose violently against me. It was high time, according to my pious confrères, to crush the neuron doctrine for good, burying at the same time its most fervent supporter. There was in their invectives so much injustice, and they were . . . so disproportionate to the insignificance of my polite observations of earlier times, that it would be ingenuous to believe that there was not a certain etiological connection between them and the award of the Nobel Prize.[41]

Personal rivalries and the clash of factions intertwined. But bitterness increased precisely because Ramón y Cajal got the credit, and leaders of competing schools did not.

Not that it always goes as planned. Once a French university awarded me an honorary doctorate. Previous experience with the ritual led me to expect that the ceremony would proceed in the usual way: we recipients would dress up in academic gowns and troop onto a stage before an audience of students and faculty, the university president would give a welcoming speech, then a faculty member (typically one who had recommended the award) would deliver a *laudatio* — literally "praise," a summary of reasons for honoring the recipient. It worked that way for my fellow candidate, Boutros Boutros-Ghali, then secretary general of the United Nations.

When my turn came, the designated faculty member delivered a blistering critique of my work. Credit had turned to blame. Shock registered on the faces of the local officials who shared the platform with me. I soon activated an all-purpose principle: convert threat into opportunity. I launched a spirited defense of the analytic line my critic had attacked. My sponsors visibly showed relief, and later apologized for the breach of protocol. Most of the time, such ceremonies proceed without trouble. They award credit in solemn ritual.

In Paris, Buenos Aires, and elsewhere, the assignment of credit and blame draws on local idioms. But it appears mainly in simplified story form. In Buenos Aires, it appears in simple stories about encounters between haughty porteños and beleaguered bolivianos. The stories often become melodramas of good guys, bad guys, and just deserts. Stories bring together claims of agency, competence, and responsibility with stipulations of the outcomes for which objects of credit or blame are responsible. They pivot on doing justice. From American courtrooms to French universities to Buenos Aires festivals, attributions of credit and blame take strikingly similar forms.

3 | CREDIT

During the turbulent year of 1929, two dramatic events occurred, with very different impacts on American life. In October a shocked country faced a stock market crash that ushered in the great depression of the 1930s. Four months earlier, on the 16th of May, the first Academy Awards ceremony took place at a banquet in the Blossom Room of Los Angeles's Hollywood Roosevelt Hotel. World War II pulled the United States out of its long depression. The Academy Awards, however, have never ceased.

The Academy of Motion Picture Arts and Sciences formed in 1927, but took two years to arrive at its winning formula. The original academy consisted of 230 people from the film industry, each paying $100 to join.[1] At first, the entire academy membership could nominate colleagues from the industry for prizes, with further screening by two tiers of judges. Soon, however, small panels of judges took over.

Three quarters of a century later, the Academy gave 24 major annual awards plus a variable number of scientific, technical, and auxiliary commendations. Its vividly televised and heavily scripted ceremony has become one of the year's major media events. Both in America and overseas, in film and other performance arts alike, the Academy Awards have spurred the highest form of compliment—imitation, right down to the use of statuettes and other icons to represent the award. France's Césars, Canada's Genies, China's Golden Roosters, and Burkina Faso's Yennenga Stallions all pay homage to Oscar.[2] The Spanish Motion Picture Academy gives its winners a bust of painter Francisco de Goya.[3] Oscar shapes film production across the world.

Philip Seymour Hoffman, who had portrayed Truman Capote in the film *Capote*, won the 2005 leading actor award for that role. As he accepted the award at the March 2006 gala, he spoke these words:

> Wow. I'm in a category with some great, great, great actors. Fantastic actors, and I'm overwhelmed. I'm really overwhelmed. I'd like to thank Bill Vince and Caroline Baron. And Danny Rosett, the film wouldn't have happened without them. I'd like to thank Sara Murphy. I'd like to thank Emily Ziff, my friends, my friends. I'd like to thank Bennett Miller, and Danny Futterman, who I love, I love, I love. You know, the Van Morrison song. I love, I love, I love, and he keeps repeating it like that. And I'd like to thank Tom Bernard, and Michael Barker. Thank you so much. And my mom's name is Marilyn O'Connor, and she's here tonight. And I'd like if you see her tonight to congratulate her. Because she brought up four kids alone, and she deserves a congratulations for that. Oh, I'm at the party, mom, you know? And she took me to my first play, and she stayed up with me and watched the NCAA final four. And my passions, her passions became my passions. And, you know, be proud, mom, because I'm proud of you, and we're here tonight, and it's so good. Thank you.[4]

Hoffman's outburst lacks the measured modesty of George Washington's farewell address. Yet, like Washington in 1798, the star of *Capote* recognized in 2006 that he had arrived at the moment for taking credit, but also—emphatically—for sharing it. Within tight time limits, awardees regularly combine expressions of amazement at their good fortune with gushing thanks to collaborators, family, and friends. They follow a standard American credit-taking script.

Not that winning the Oscar ever comes as a complete surprise. In recent years, screening panels have nominated three to five candidates for each major award, and the nominees have decked themselves out in formal dress for the spectacle. What's more, studios and individual performers have regularly campaigned for nominations. Film critic, Oscar specialist, and Columbia University sociology Ph.D. Emanuel Levy tells the following story:

> In 1945, Joan Crawford and her press agent, Henry Rogers, conducted one of the biggest campaigns in Hollywood history. According to biographer Bob Thomas, during the filming of *Mildred Pierce*, producer Jerry Wald sensed that something extraordinary was happening, upon which he called Rogers and suggested:
>
> > WALD: Why don't you start a campaign for Joan to win the Oscar?
> >
> > ROGERS: But Jerry, the picture is just starting.
> >
> > WALD: So?
> >
> > ROGERS: So how would I go about it?
> >
> > WALD: It's simple. Call up Hedda Hopper and tell her, "Joan Crawford is giving such a strong performance in *Mildred Pierce* that her fellow-workers are already predicting that she'll win the Oscar for it."

ROGERS: Jerry, you're full of shit.
WALD: Possibly. But it might work. What have you
got to lose?

In his daily reports to the famous gossip columnist, Rogers delivered some "confidential" reports. A few days later, Hopper wrote: "Insiders say that Joan Crawford is delivering such a terrific performance in *Mildred Pierce* that she's a cinch for the Academy Awards." Other columnists followed Hopper, all predicting an Oscar for Crawford.[5]

The following spring, Joan Crawford won the 1945 best actress award for her performance in *Mildred Pierce*.

Levy sums up the place of Academy Awards in recent American culture:

Is it too much to suggest that standing on the Oscar podium and thanking your family and friends—and every person you have ever met in your life—has become the ultimate American fantasy? The strong need to be recognized, the urge to be acknowledged in public, the desire to grab the spotlight. Not for fifteen minutes of fame, as Andy Warhol predicted in the 1960s—that's too long. A forty-five-second speech, which is the Academy's prescribed norm, will do, or swelling music will interrupt your speech in mid-sentence. Unless, of course, you're Julia Roberts or Warren Beatty, whose speeches have been some of the longest in Oscar's history.[6]

Jane Wyman brought down the average time in 1949 when she accepted the award for her part as a deaf-mute in *Johnny Belinda*. Her entire speech ran as follows: "I accept this very gratefully for keeping my mouth shut for once. I think I'll do it again."[7] On the whole, however, Oscar winners have filled their 45 seconds of immortality with words, words, words. Like victorious finalists at Wimbledon or the World Cup, they have won their matches, and arrived at glory.

Remember how credit works. Whether someone (like Julia Roberts or Warren Beatty) is taking credit or someone else (like the 2006 Oscar host, comedian Jon Stewart) is giving credit, they are claiming that the recipient did something that actually caused an increase in the value of an important activity. The best actress in a leading role outdid her competitors in adding to the value of her film. What's more, she wasn't simply the creature of circumstances or other people's help: through deliberate deployment of her talent, she caused a better film to come out.

As the acceptance speech's references to collaborators, friends, and family indicates, furthermore, taking or giving credit draws a line between deserving insiders and everyone else. Participants in taking or giving credit package credit's elements—competence, responsibility, outcome, and us-them boundary—in recognizable stories. If someone deviates too far from that script, someone else always pops up to correct them. At least off-screen, furthermore, some rival or some member of an excluded faction usually complains that the wrong person or faction got the credit. This chapter shows how those crucial elements of credit fit together.

Humans have invented four different ways of fitting the elements together: tournaments, honors, promotions, and networks.

- In *tournaments*, a process of competitive elimination starts with plenty of candidates but ends with only one winner—an individual or a team—in each category.

- In *honors*, present members of a select group accept nominations of current outsiders from other members, and organize a screening process to decide who is worthy to join them.

- In *promotions*, a whole class of people who have reached a certain rank goes through some sort of screening that determines which of them advances into the next higher rank.

- In *networks*, people draw on local scripts and resources to distinguish people whose performances deserve credit.

Tournaments, honors, promotions, and networks all build justice detectors. In all four modes, the givers and claimers of credit are declaring that someone—or a bunch of someones—has added value to some significant activity through competent, responsible performance. They are saying that the performance puts the receiver of credit on the good side of an us-them boundary. It also puts the giver of credit on the same side as the receiver.

The categories overlap a bit. For example, in some honorary societies an elite board of judges selects the newcomers, more like a tournament. In others, the whole membership votes on who can join them, yet sometimes a single member can blackball a candidate. The Oscars amount to an annual tournament, but membership in the Academy of Motion Picture Arts and Sciences comes closer to the honors model. School graduations typically involve promotions, although in some elite schools they also borrow from honors. Promotions within ranked organizations usually operate more selectively than school graduations; some members get them, most don't. In that regard, they come closer to tournaments and honors than school graduations do. Everyday awarding of credit, however, rarely follows the patterns of tournaments, honors, or promotions. Instead, it depends on storytelling within local networks.

TOURNAMENTS

My Columbia University colleague Eric Kandel shared the Nobel Prize for Physiology or Medicine. His powerful memoir *In Search of Memory* chronicles the life and work that produced his discoveries concerning how memory operates. It begins with his family's flight from Vienna in 1938 as the Nazis took over, and ends with the prize's aftermath. On Yom Kippur 2000, he tells us, his New York telephone rang at 5:15 AM. The Nobel Foundation's secretary general was calling to tell him about the prize. Comments Kandel:

> The Stockholm deliberations must be among the best-kept secrets in the world. There are practically never any leaks. As a result, it is almost impossible to know who will get the prize in any given October. Yet very few people who receive the Nobel Prize are absolutely astonished by the very idea of winning it. Most people who are eligible sense that they are being considered because their colleagues speak of the possibility. Moreover, the Karolinska Institute runs periodic symposia designed to bring the world's leading biologists to Stockholm, and I had just attended such a symposium a few weeks earlier. Nonetheless I had not expected this call. Many eminently prizeworthy candidates who are talked about as being eligible are never selected as laureates, and I thought it unlikely that I would be recognized.[8]

Kandel is describing his arrival at a tournament's top. Like Oscar winners, he takes pains to share the credit. Yet he also recognizes that his scientific performance was "prizeworthy."

You might think that the world of academic prizes stands aloof from the tournament-style campaigning that regularly besets the Oscars and other entertainment awards like it. But here's what an economist from the Swedish Academy told me in 1996. The Swedish Academy awards the Nobel Prizes in economics. It gets the money from the Swedish Riksbank rather than the Nobel Foundation. That doesn't devalue the prize, or make contenders less eager to win it. "We have no trouble," laughed the economist, "getting promising economists to speak in Stockholm. In fact, they're often willing to pay their own way." No Hedda Hopper publishes the gossip of economics. But there and elsewhere in academia plenty of discreet politicking surrounds major prizes.

Should we be surprised? Even organizations that tend to promote and reward people on the basis of competent performance and staying out of trouble rather than individual brilliance usually award them signs that they have made it up through the ranks. My performance as a junior U.S. Navy officer during the Korean War won me nothing more than medals for good conduct and for service during the Korean emergency. But it got me a promotion before I fled definitively—and gratefully—to civilian life. It even yielded some civilian benefits. I went back to school on the GI Bill. Now, if my civilian health insurance fails, I can still turn to the Veterans Administration for care. I won no tournaments or admissions to military honorary societies during my service. On my uniform, nevertheless, I proudly wore the ribbons that stood for those two medals and the stripes that stood for my rank. They showed that I wasn't an absolute greenhorn.

Most of the plentiful ribbons you see on the chests of high-ranking military officers stand for trouble-free service rather than bravery under fire. Perform competently, stay out of trouble, and most of the time you'll receive a promotion along with others in your cohort. Still, above a certain rank— say, colonel for most military forces—promotion structure shifts. It moves from relatively gradual attrition between one rank and the next higher to sharp competition for advancement. Above that point, military promotion turns into a tournament: a structure with a broad base and a narrow peak.

The worlds in which prizes count most resemble tournaments. Consider the worlds of novelists, poets, painters, dancers, runners, violinists, boxers, opera singers, fashion models, jazz musicians, and motion picture actors. Tournaments seduce. They offer spectacular rewards to a few highly visible winners, and stimulate excessive hopes among likely losers.[9] They involve innumerable participants, part time or full time, at the lower ranks, but only a handful who receive recognition at the top.

Although some people stick with these competitive activities for the pleasure, the adventure, or the scent of blood, most never receive the credit they think they deserve. My own world of American academia is a bit more benign. A competent performer often moves up rank by rank without ever becoming famous or winning big prizes. But at its higher levels, like military services, academia shifts to tournament structures. Within an elite, competition for credit, including prizes up to and including Nobel Prizes, becomes acute and sometimes fierce.

A negative example proves the point. In 2002, Russian mathematician Grigory Perelman began publishing proofs of a conjecture by Frenchman Henri Poincaré, who died in 1912. The conjecture concerns characteristics of three-dimensional spheres. Not only had the proof eluded mathematicians for a century, but the Clay Mathematics Institute had announced a million-dollar prize for a valid solution to the problem. Building on the work of my Columbia colleague Richard Hamilton, Perelman proposed an unconventional, sophisticated solution. By 2006, knowledgeable mathematicians across the world had validated Perelman's proof.

A committee of the International Mathematical Union voted to award forty-year-old Perelman a Fields Medal, the world's chief recognition for mathematicians forty and younger. Yet Chinese-American mathematician Shing-Tung Yau (himself an earlier winner of the Fields Medal for his work on what came to be called Calabi-Yau manifolds) challenged Perelman's priority. Yau, who himself had built on the work of Eugenio Calabi, argued that his students Xi-Ping Zhu and Huai-Dong Cao had provided the definitive proof. Specialist Dan Stroock of MIT complained:

> "Calabi outlined a program," Stroock said. "In a real sense, Yau was Calabi's Perelman. Now he's on the other side. He's had no compunction at all in taking the lion's share of credit for Calabi-Yau. And now he seems to be resenting Perelman getting credit for completing Hamilton's program. I don't know if the analogy has ever occurred to him."[10]

Perelman turned the tables on everyone. He refused the Fields Medal, failed to apply for the million-dollar prize, and retired to his small research center in St. Petersburg, Russia. Yet in this particular fierce tournament, it seems likely that historians of mathematics will declare him the winner—give him the credit. In a letter to the *New Yorker*, Stroock added a qualifying comment on Perelman and Yau: "Of course, the rest of us are jealous of their immortality, but our jealousy does not excuse our succumbing to the crab-bucket syndrome."[11] Crabs in a bucket claw and chew each other up instead of respectfully awarding credit to the best among them. Academic tournaments often turn into crab buckets.

HONORS

If you went through the American educational system, your high school or prep school probably had a dean's list and a chapter of the National Honor Society. My high school did. If so, your school transcript most likely showed that you won both honors. (After all, you're reading this book, which probably means you did well in school.) For the NHS, you received a small gold pin to wear. It signaled that you had accumulated a high grade point average, then passed screening by a faculty committee. The committee was also supposed to consider service, leadership, character, and citizenship before letting you through the screen. These days the NHS sets its standard at a cumulative 85 percent grade or the equivalent.[12]

For a while, I proudly wore the NHS pin on my lapel. Then I went to college. I soon learned that almost all my American classmates had received NHS membership, and many of them far greater distinctions. The pin disappeared into the drawer containing cufflinks and charms. Something similar happened a few years later, as my Phi Beta Kappa key went into storage when I entered an academic world largely populated by people carrying the same key. How much credit membership in an honorary society gets you obviously depends on the setting in which you flaunt the membership.

Unlike the bulk of honorary societies, the NHS relies on adult screeners rather than the existing membership for its work of co-optation. Phi Beta Kappa gives chapters the choice between relying on a local faculty committee and allowing current student members to join the judges. In most systems of honors, however, previously selected members decide who is worthy to join them. Several effects follow:

- Existing members more often select newcomers who are already connected to them;

- existing members more often select newcomers who resemble them;

- factionalized honor groups either recruit newcomers to support their dominant factions or divide newcomers among existing factions; and therefore,

- honorary societies usually reproduce themselves from one recruitment round to the next.

Consider those high-prestige honorary societies called national academies. Since the seventeenth century, most western countries have created academies of letters, sciences, medicine, and other intellectual pursuits. The first western European academies drew on Greek, Roman, and Italian Renaissance models, but gave them local spins. France's Cardinal Richelieu created the most prestigious early modern academy in 1635. Then chief minister for King Louis XIII, he turned an informal salon of literati who had been meeting privately for several years to hear each other's papers and conversation into a royal institution: the Académie Française. The new academy received responsibility for guaranteeing the purity of the French language.

In that day of patronage, no one could create such an institution without incorporating grandees who enjoyed high rank without necessarily possessing literary talent or grammatical skill. As a seventeenth-century chronicler of the academy's founding put it delicately:

> One of the first conditions was that these gentlemen add to their company a number of meritorious people, some of whom qualified by their social rank. Since the Court always adopts the preferences of ministers and royal favorites with enthusiasm, especially when the preferences are reasonable and upright, those who were closest to the Cardinal, and who had reputations for sharp wits, took pride in joining a corps of which he was the protector and father.[13]

Since that time, the French head of state—chief minister, king, emperor, or president—has always received the title "protector" of the Academy.

After Louis XIII's initial appointments, the French Academy set a pattern: forty members elected for life except for egregious misconduct, new members selected by existing members after soliciting membership and courting those existing members, glorious meeting halls, grand ceremonies of admission including inaugural speeches and eulogies, enormous prestige. Aside from meetings for mutual admiration and celebration, the Academy publishes the definitive dictionary of the French language, now in its ninth edition since initial publication in 1694.

Academies multiplied in France. Paris itself soon acquired the:

- Academy of Painting and Sculpture (1648)
- Academy of Inscriptions and Belles-Lettres (1663)

- Academy of Sciences (1666)

- Academy of Music (1669)

Under minister Jean-Baptiste Colbert's influence, for example, the Academy of Sciences gave royal recognition to an elite group of mathematicians and natural scientists. King Louis XIV and his successors continued to make the Academy's formal appointments, especially to honorary rather than working memberships. But increasingly Academy members selected their new members. Their choices had powerful effects, because the Academy acquired the rights to approve scientific projects, make appointments to specialized scientific bodies, advise the government on scientific decisions, and monopolize major positions in teaching and research.[14]

Major French cities soon started imitating Paris. By 1700, Angers, Arles, Avignon, Caen, Lyon, Nîmes, Soissons, Toulouse, and Villefranche-en-Beaujolais had their own academies, most of them affiliated with the French Academy.[15] The great historian of French provincial academies Daniel Roche points out how much they became part of royal absolutism, with its project of defining French culture from Paris and Versailles. Their members spoke and advocated Parisian French as they promoted Parisian culture.

"In 18th century society," remarks Roche,

the monarchy could call on the cultured class to be a ruling class. It thus confirmed the idea of a society organized around service and merit. For nobles who divided by origins, seniority, function, and wealth, it proposed reconciliation in cultural action. To separate bourgeoisies, it offered a shared calling of sacrifice and (in the name of social benefit and service to the state) reconciliation between the worlds of leisure and trade. The academic ideal could thus become an expression of enlightened absolutism in building a new social order and managing the old society of divided Estates.[16]

The French academies projected an ideal picture of the self-selected honorary society: distinction in the service of humanity.

That very distinction promoted competition for membership. In 1683 and 1684, for example, Jean de la Fontaine became a candidate for the French Academy. Author of the *Fables* people still read today, he then attracted opposition from the Academy's clergy for his scandalous secularism. They preferred Nicolas Boileau, a rival, very Catholic poet who served as "historiographer" to King Louis XIV. Louis was at that very time dramatizing his claim to be the ideal Catholic monarch by stepping up persecution of France's remaining Protestants.[17] The king delayed la Fontaine's nomination by six months, then inserted Boileau into the Academy on his own authority later in 1684.

As years went on, however, protectors intervened less and less in the self-selection of academy members. As a result, newcomers increasingly resembled the old-timers who elected them. The resemblance included gender: only four women have ever occupied places in the academy. The first among them, the Franco-American Marguerite Yourcenar, only took her seat in 1980. In France as elsewhere, "distinction" has its limits. In honorary societies, those limits come largely from the self-images of existing members.

The ideal picture projected by academies caught on well outside of France. During the American Civil War, a coalition of scientists, engineers, and military officers used the emergency to promote formation of a prestigious body that could eventually rival the French Academy of Sciences:

> Three leading government scientists, hoping to make a place for science in the war effort, got the Navy Department to appoint them in February 1863 as a "Permanent Commission" to advise it on scientific and technological matters. Unpaid and unfunded, the commission merely evaluated such outside proposals as were referred to it, without significant results. The same trio and two others, having long yearned for an American equivalent of the French Academy of Sciences, also seized the wartime opportunity to wangle a congressional charter for a National Academy of Sciences on the grounds that it could dispense such counsel to the government generally. Being likewise unfunded and also weakened by an uproar over the naming of members, the new academy was ignored by the government, though it became prestigious and influential in the next century.[18]

The NAS survived. It eventually occupied a triple role in American intellectual life. It advised different branches of government on scientific issues. It became a public voice of science on controversial questions such as today's discussions of global warming and biological evolution. And it singled out a select minority of scientists both by inducting them into membership and by awarding prizes to a smaller number of them. In addition to awarding membership and prizes, the NAS started convening committees, issuing reports, and holding well-publicized meetings on matters of scientific debate.

These days the NAS has about 1,800 members, who elect seventy or eighty new scientists each year to replace those who die. It also works with two parallel academies: the National Academy of Engineering and the Institute of Medicine. The three of them operate a joint research arm, the National Research Council. Far larger than their French equivalents, these academies still broadcast the ideal of distinction in the service of humanity. They, too, co-opt new members who mostly resemble old members. NAS social scientists co-opted me in 1983. Since then, I have done my share of committee work, report writing, and attendance at meetings on one issue or another. I have also played my part in co-opting newcomers. On the average, the newcomers resemble the people who already belong, including me.

Every award of honors, however local and humble, does some version of the same. The model gives credit by plucking new people from some pool of eligibles and making them members of a self-selected elite. It moves the newcomers across an us-them boundary. It gives them credit for competence and responsibility that produced such a desirable outcome: the superior performance that qualified them for membership.

PROMOTIONS

Promotions also award credit for responsible, superior performance. But promotions less regularly involve induction into a self-selected elite. Instead, supposedly competent judges declare that the eligible people have collectively met standards for movement to the next higher grade.

Judges, candidates, and third parties connected to one or the other often care intensely about whether the candidates have actually met the announced standards. In his 1999 State of the Union Address, U.S. president Bill Clinton called for an end of what he called "social promotion," moving unqualified children from one grade to the next on the basis of age alone. The U.S. Department of Education soon issued a report called *Taking Responsibility for Ending Social Promotion.* The report declared:

> To pass students along in school when they are unprepared or retain them without addressing their needs denies students access to opportunities at the next level of schooling, in postsecondary education, and in the workplace. Both policies send a message to students that little is expected from them, that they have little worth, and that they do not warrant the time and effort it would take to help them be successful in school. The cost of these policies extends beyond individual students to society as a whole. Employers have little confidence in a high school diploma as proof that graduates are prepared with the requisite skills. Colleges and businesses spend resources providing remedial training for students and employees. Lack of education and skills is highly associated with poverty, crime, and violence among youth and young adults.[19]

Social promotion, Secretary of Education Richard Riley declared, had become a national problem. It was undermining the significance of high school diplomas. It was dissolving the connection between performance and credit.

School graduations, in contrast, dramatize that very connection. In Canada and the United States, high school and college graduation ceremonies follow a standard pattern. What happens?

- Graduates who have passed the basic requirements dress up in medieval-looking caps and gowns, all of roughly the same color and style. (In colleges and universities, the costumes' hoods—never worn as hoods!—vary by specialty and rank of degree.)

- Family and friends also dress up, but not in caps and gowns, and take seats in a ceremonial space.

- As the audience rises, graduates march into the space, often to music such as Elgar's *Pomp and Circumstance March No. 1*, and frequently led by costumed dignitaries.

- Graduates and audience sit down.

- One or more speakers (sometimes including representatives of the graduates) give talks.

- Officials give out honors to graduates, teachers, and/or special guests.

- Graduates file across the space one by one to receive diplomas (or reasonable facsimiles) as someone reads their names.

- One of the officials pronounces them graduated.

- The officials and graduates march out before the audience disbands.

- Parties begin.

In quasi-religious form, the ceremony bestows credit collectively.

The resemblance to religious ceremonies should not surprise us. North American graduation exercises still follow rituals from the European fourteenth century, when the only students to receive formal degrees belonged to religious orders, and studied with priests. For six centuries, commencements have signaled that a whole class of students has met basic requirements and is now moving on to the next phase in life. As in tournaments and honorary societies, the class receives credit for responsible performance that produced the successful outcome: value added to the individual's knowledge and skills. But in a commencement most or all of the eligible people have passed that test at more or less the same time. They have moved on to join previous generations. Like fourteenth-century clerics who became doctors of theology, they rise to a higher grade.

More goes on in graduation ceremonies than aping ancestors. Sometimes, for example, the commencement speaker even says something clever. When India-born Indra Nooyi, president and chief financial officer of PepsiCo, addressed the Columbia University Business School graduating class in May 2005, she offered the analogy of the continents with the fingers of a hand. She identified the long middle finger with the United States: if used inappropriately, she went on to say,

> just like the U.S. itself—the middle finger can convey a negative message and get us in trouble. You know what I'm talking about. In fact, I suspect you're hoping that I'll demonstrate what I mean. And trust me, I'm not looking for volunteers to model.
>
> Discretion being the better part of valor . . . I think I'll pass.
>
> What is most crucial to my analogy of the five fingers as the five major continents, is that each of us in the U.S.—the long middle finger—must be careful that when we extend our arm in either a business or political sense, we take pains to assure we are giving a hand . . .

not the finger. Sometimes this is very difficult. Because the U.S.—the middle finger—sticks out so much, we can send the wrong message unintentionally.

Unfortunately, I think this is how the rest of the world looks at the U.S. right now. Not as part of the hand—giving strength and purpose to the rest of the fingers—but, instead, scratching our nose and sending a far different signal.[20]

Here are instructions for a commencement speaker: Say something lively and at least mildly hortatory. Be brief—remember that cocktail parties can only begin when the ceremony ends. And give the graduates credit. Package their distinctive competence, responsibility, outcome, and us-them boundary in a recognizable story. Indra Nooyi did all these things, then went one better. She gave the graduates' elders credit: "Each of your parents," she concluded, "believes that their hard work has paid off. Finally! They believe that maybe—just maybe—they have raised and nurtured the next Jack Welch, Meg Whitman, or Patricia Russo."[21] The next time I speak at a graduation, I'll try to emulate Indra Nooyi.

Promotions only feature graduation ceremonies when whole classes of persons pass similar obstacles at about the same time. A far wider range of promotions award credit more individually. Like schools, they divide people into grades, but people move from one grade to the next at their own pace, and sometimes not at all. In big graded organizations, nevertheless, workers ordinarily expect some sort of promotion if they perform reasonably at their jobs, stick around, and stay out of trouble. They get credit for serving the organization.

My father certainly thought so. Dad had dropped out of high school to support his family when a tractor-factory accident had crippled his father, my grandfather. Dad then went to night school, received a high school diploma, did further courses in accounting, and eventually worked his way up through several white collar ranks. A few years after I got a Ph.D. and started university teaching, Dad took me aside. "You've had a good education, and seem to be bright enough," he said. "How come you're not a dean yet?" To my father, "dean" meant "boss."

I had to explain: universities had another promotion system. If you performed reasonably at your job, stuck to it, and stayed out of trouble, eventually you would move from instructor to assistant professor to associate professor to professor. You wouldn't necessarily ever serve as dean. As it turned out, the universities I worked for finally made me a professor, but never named me dean. They gave me credit as a scholar and teacher, not as an administrator.

CONTESTED PROMOTIONS

Sociologists often look closely at ranked promotion systems like the ones that operate in North American colleges and universities. Such systems give sociologists an unusual opportunity to apply their statistical skills to problems the people involved care about: Who gets promoted, and who doesn't? The statistical analysis can run either or both of two ways. You can ask what attributes and performances the system rewards with promotion. You can also ask whether the system systematically rewards some categories of candidates, and systematically penalizes others.

In the second sort of analysis, the statistical treatment typically factors out variables such as educational level, job experience, and performance ratings, then determines whether some significant portion of the remaining variation in promotion correlates with membership or non-membership in the suspected category: race, gender, or something else. Roughly speaking, it asks whether the system is sorting people by race, gender, or some other categorical membership when they are otherwise similarly qualified for promotion.

This sort of statistical analysis has two drawbacks. First, it involves a narrow view of discrimination: differences in outcomes for people who are similar except for their categorical memberships. Educational level, job experience, performance ratings, and other attributes often result from categorical membership, but in such an analysis they don't count as part of discrimination. Second, it says little or nothing about the processes that cause the differential outcomes by category: direct rejection of promotion candidates by bosses, differences in previous job assignments, sabotage by work associates, or other obstacles to advancement? Still, their stark, conservative nature helps such statistical analyses spotlight differences that call out for explanation.[22] They build justice detectors that ask whether some classes of agents get less reward for their responsibility and competence than other classes of agents do.

Just such analyses figure in a court case concerning sex discrimination in American Wal-Mart stores. In the United States, retail trade follows a pattern that Karl Marx made famous: it offers capitalists the opportunity to get richer as their employees get poorer. Over the last few decades, discounting, cost-cutting, and cutthroat competition have made large-scale retail trade very profitable. They have also made it a major sector of declining relative wages. The expansion of large-scale retail trade has contributed significantly to the country's overall rise in income inequality.[23]

Wal-Mart led the whole industry. By the early twenty-first century, Wal-Mart had become the world's largest private employer and America's richest corporation. It had also become the object of a class action lawsuit destined to make waves, *Dukes, et al. v. Wal-Mart Stores, Inc.* In 2001, seven female current and former employees, including Betty Dukes, sued Wal-Mart under the Civil Rights Act of 1964. They complained about discrimination in wages, job assignments, and promotion. Big cases move slowly. In June 2004, San Francisco federal district court judge Martin Jenkins ruled that the case could become a class action on behalf of all the company's present and former female employees. That meant a possible 1.6 million beneficiaries, the largest class action suit ever accepted by American courts.

Attorneys for the women hired three experts: economist Marc Bendick, sociologist William Bielby, and statistician Richard Drogin. Bendick concentrated on the representation of women in Wal-Mart management, Bielby on Wal-Mart personnel practices, Drogin on women's hiring, firing, and job-to-job movement within Wal-Mart. Of the three, Drogin's analysis centered most directly on promotion discrimination. Most of the time it distinguished among three clusters of jobs: entry-level assignments within stores (paid hourly wages), store management (paid salaries plus bonuses), and above-store management (likewise paid salaries plus bonuses).

The plaintiffs' lead attorney Brad Seligman summarized Wal-Mart's management promotion ladder for the district court:

> You go from support manager to management trainee, assistant manager, co-manager, store manager. It's the same progression that you move up the line. And as you go up that line, there is increasing responsibility. It's also clear in the record that in the absence of the

store manager, the co-manager acts. In the absence of the co-manager, the assistant manager acts. And in the absence of the assistant manager, the support manager acts. So it's a question of degree, going up the line.[24]

The boundary between hourly employees and salaried management separated management trainees from assistant managers, who got their jobs after four to six months of traineeship.

In 2001, women made up 70 percent of Wal-Mart's hourly employees, while only 33 percent of salaried employees were women. Almost 90 percent of all customer service managers (the lowest-level supervisory job) were women, while about 15 percent of all store managers were female. Within each major category, furthermore, women received significantly less pay than men.[25] The experts activated their statistical justice detectors. They asked whether the system of job assignments feeding into management traineeships systematically set women aside. Did Wal-Mart women receive less credit for their value-adding performances than men did for similar performances? In the lawsuit's early stages, the experts were also asking whether Wal-Mart's job assignment, promotion, and payment policies were sufficiently uniform and centralized for all female employees to constitute a single legal class.

The experts' answer to both questions: yes. All the analyses pointed in the same direction. Despite the fact that women stayed at Wal-Mart longer than men and received higher average performance ratings, Wal-Mart promoted fewer women than men at every rank, promoted women more slowly, and paid them less after promotion. Moreover, Wal-Mart did not post new management openings within stores. Instead, the company relied on existing managers to spot likely candidates as openings arose. As former employee Detrx Young told interviewers:

> Sometime in 1998, I wrote on my evaluation that I would like to be promoted to Support Manager [an hourly position]. I had overheard someone say that the position would be open, so I put it on the evaluation to show my interest . . . By that time, I had been with the company for seven years and had worked in nearly every department. I was very familiar with the store and the procedures, and I was willing to work at any time, any hour. I really wanted to move up with this company. Despite talking to my Assistant Manager and putting my name on the list, I was never even interviewed. Instead, they promoted a male named John Cooper who had less seniority, less experience, and had not put his name on the list in the break room. John Cooper was promoted by the Store Manager, Mr. Glen Flory, with whom he was friendly.[26]

Young and her counterparts at Wal-Mart were not getting full credit for their job performances. On the contrary, they were receiving penalties for belonging to the wrong social category. As I write in the spring of 2007, no one knows how and when the huge legal case will end. But the contest clearly pivots on our main question: Does this sort of promotion system give full credit to the performances of people who belong to disfavored categories? The answer, it seems, is no.

NETWORKS

Philip Roth published his meditation on fleshly mortality, *Everyman*, in 2006. The novel begins with the funeral of the unnamed antihero: everyman. After a life punctuated by three marriages, two children, a string of love affairs, a career in advertising, and increasing health crises, everyman has died in surgery on his right carotid artery, At the funeral, his rich, infuriatingly healthy older brother Howie talks about their days in their father's Elizabeth, New Jersey, jewelry store. He describes the Christian girls their father hired, and how his little brother would work with them. The now-dead brother would impress the girls by counting envelopes with his fast, dexterous fingers. He took pride in working for his father. "How that boy," continues Howie,

> loved doing everything that went along with being the jeweler's reliable son! That was our father's favorite accolade—"reliable."[27]

Most of the time, most of us get our credit in similar small ways. Within a known network, we acquire reputations for responsible competence that somehow contributes to a valued enterprise. We take care of our friends, make people laugh, sacrifice so that other people will live better, and so on. When my father died, we grieving children sat around my sister Carolyn's Illinois living room with stacks of old family photographs. Holding up favorite pictures, we told stories of half-remembered events involving Mom and Dad. We gave both of them credit for bringing us through the Depression, sending us to college, and the thousand other services that parents perform for their children. We wept as we recalled a life now past.

Most networks lack the grandeur of the circuits that run tournaments and honors. Few of them have the formal organization of a promotion system. Yet through gossip, social pressure, and moral discussion they play crucial parts in the awarding of credit. They provide reassurance that we have performed worthily and served whichever "us" they represent. Of course the very same networks assign us blame when others think we have let them down. Whatever else they do, local networks process credit and blame.

Even more so than in tournaments, honors, and promotions, rules for credit in networks vary greatly with local cultures. In all four types of credit, awards for credit distinguish insiders from outsiders, and identify current recipients of credit with the insiders. In all four systems, participants generally recognize scripts for good and bad behavior. But how those scripts sort people out varies.

In all tournaments, far more people start at the competition's bottom than end up winning, and each stage of competition eliminates a significant share of the candidates. At that end of the range, furthermore, the rules tend to be fairly public, uniform, and unchanging. As we move through honors and promotions to networks, those features change. At the network end, many winners survive to receive credit, while the standards remain fuzzier, more variable, and changeable as a result of local cultures and negotiations among network members.

Networks award credit to many members on the basis of local rules. As a result, insiders may well understand the bases for credit-giving intuitively, while outsiders find them mystifying. Promotions generally involve more public, uniform rules even if gender discrimination or favoritism occurs. On the whole, promotions produce fewer winners than networks. Yet on the average more winners receive credit in promotions than in honors or, especially, tournaments. In honors and tournaments, the rules for winning usually become more general and visible than in promotions and, especially, in networks. Obviously exceptions apply: secret societies, for example, often tap new members on the basis of rules they would never divulge to the public. Still, in general the scope and visibility of rules for receiving credit rise as the number of winners declines.

As a result, networks often maintain sharp contrasts between their internal awards of credit and standards that prevail outside the network. Honor among thieves illustrates the contrast. Timothy Gilfoyle has written a beguiling biography of New York pickpocket, confidence man, stage actor, and (eventually) informer George Appo. More exactly, he has taken the unpublished autobiography Appo wrote in his fifties, amplifying it with heroic historical investigation of Appo's record and context.

Born to a Chinese immigrant father and an Irish immigrant mother in 1856, Appo became famous as a superior criminal who survived many a fight as he moved in and out of prison. He ended up with one eye gone and his body full of bullets. After he left New York's Matteawan State Hospital for the Criminally Insane in 1899, Appo became an undercover agent for crime investigators in the high-minded Society for the Prevention of Crime (SPC). By that time, he had lost his credit among his partners in crime.

For a quarter of a century, nevertheless, George Appo received grudging admiration from fellow criminals, including many of the police who played both sides of the line. After going straight, he drew credit from the reformers for whom he worked during his post-prison years. As Gilfoyle sums up:

> Rather than being Catholic, Irish, or Chinese, Appo was a "good fellow," someone who displayed courage— a "nervy crook"—while at the same time using wit and guile to make a living and lavishing the proceeds on others—"a money getter and spender." Most important,

a good fellow accepted the consequences of his actions, even serving prison time "for some other fellow's evil doing," according to Appo. SPC superintendent Howard Barber described Appo as "loyal to the core," adding that the reformed convict "was one of the most fearless men I have ever known."[27]

We might, to be sure, conclude that Appo challenges the localism of network rules for giving credit. Good fellows attract admiration in many different settings. But look again: who gave Appo credit and why depended tightly on his performance within his current network—first fellow criminals, then their enemies. Appo offers the exception that proves the rule.

In networks, promotions, honors, and tournaments alike, insiders tell stories about receivers of credit. The stories vary wildly in the outcomes they emphasize as well as in the performances they say produced the outcomes. Being a "good fellow" differs dramatically from making great scientific discoveries. Yet credit-giving stories share a common structure. In all stories, responsible, competent performance produced an increase in the value of an activity that insiders share and value. Recognition of the performance sharpens the boundary between worthy insiders and less worthy outsiders. It dramatizes a moral division of the social world.

4 | BLAME

In 2003, the 20th of February brought consuming fire to West Warwick, Rhode Island. That night the rock band Great White performed at the West Warwick nightclub The Station, owned by brothers Michael and Jeffrey Derderian. As the band played, band manager Daniel Biechele lighted fireworks. The club's polyurethane foam insulation instantly burst into flames. The fire killed 100 people. Beset by civil suits on behalf of fire victims, the Derderian brothers filed for bankruptcy in November 2005. In 2006, Rhode Island courts sentenced Biechele to four years in prison for involuntary manslaughter. The Derderian brothers pled no contest to similar charges. Michael, 46, received a sentence of four years in a minimum-security prison, while Jeffrey, 39, got 500 hours of community service and three years' probation.

Associate Justice Francis Darigan of the Rhode Island State Superior Court sentenced the Derderians. At the hearing's start, Darigan projected photos of the dead on a large courtroom screen. He then declared to an emotional courtroom crowd that "My greatest regret, my most sincere regret is that this criminal justice system cannot give you the relief you seek, cannot assuage your grief."

Nevertheless, the victims' relatives vigorously condemned the light sentences:

> "I can no longer pledge allegiance to a flag that has no guarantee of liberty and justice for all," said Claire Bruyere, whose daughter was killed, one of more than 25 victims' relatives who spoke in court. "I was born an American citizen. Now I wish I could give that citizenship back."[1]

Gina Russo, whose fiancé died in the fire, had spent eleven weeks in a coma with burns on her head and arms. She now wore a wig to cover her scars. "You have done us a great disservice," she complained to Justice Darigan. "We were owed a trial. I waited three and a half years for this. This is my life sentence. I have to look at myself every day."[2] The judge silenced testifying relatives when they moved from their personal grief to complaints about the sentences. He encouraged their mourning of losses, but not their objections to his management of the case.

Sons of a Warwick grocery store owner, the Derderian brothers grew up in Rhode Island. Michael Derderian became a local businessman as the younger Jeffrey went to Rhode Island College before working as a radio-television broadcaster in Boston and Providence. In 2000, the pair bought the West Warwick nightclub then called The Filling Station, renaming it The Station. They responded to neighbors' complaints about noise by lining the club with egg crate insulation made of polyurethane. As it happened, Jeffrey aired a broadcast about the flammability of polyurethane foam on Boston's WHDH-TV in 2001. Yet the brothers claimed not to have known that they had put polyurethane on their walls. They had the insulation painted a dark color. Fire inspectors didn't notice it either.[3]

At the sentencing, the Derderian brothers voiced deep regret:

> "This tragedy has our name on it," said Jeffrey Derderian, who was in the club the night of the fire and dissolved in tears reading from a hand-scrawled statement.
>   "There are many days I wish I didn't make it out of that building because if I didn't maybe some families would feel better," he said. "I know many of you would have liked it if I died, too. I hear the screams, the broken glass, the terror of that night in my head."[4]

Worse yet, the brothers had started to sell the nightclub when the fire occurred. They had scheduled a transfer of their liquor license for the next day. Michael Derderian's wife Heather was already suing him for divorce, pressing him to sell the club to make a settlement and meet their mounting debts.[5] The Derderian brothers had plenty of reasons for regret. With the band's manager, they took the blame.

This chapter asks and answers two questions about blame: How do people who have witnessed or suffered a loss go about assigning blame? What do they treat as adequate compensation for the loss? It arrives at a surprising conclusion. Blame results from social processes very similar to those that produce credit, but now turned upside down. In the assignment of blame, the justice detector follows the same general principles as in assigning credit, but produces opposite results. The chapter shows how the process works for culpable negligence, harm to children, drug-related crime, and responsibility for the 9/11 terror attacks.

In all these cases, blamers estimate the loss in value of some important activity, including the activity of a human life. They judge the competence and responsibility of actors for the loss. They weigh the loss for that competence and responsibility, and seek compensation equal to the weighted loss. If they have suffered the loss themselves, they demand recognition of their victimization. Like givers of credit, they draw a clear line between us and them—between the worthy sufferers and the unworthy remainder. They become indignant if authorities assign too light a penalty, or say that no one was to blame. They ask for justice in something like the old *lex talionis*: an eye for an eye, a tooth for a tooth, tit for tat.

By their own standards, they don't always get justice. The law works with statutes, precedents, and stylized categories. Although (as the Derderian case shows us) plenty of emotion erupts in courtrooms, judges try to keep decisions on the unemotional tracks of existing codes. They steer discussion away from popular justice toward what a "reasonable person" would do in the circumstances. Novelist and law professor Thane Rosenbaum complains about that standard:

> After all, while the reasonable man, through sheer moral blindness and undaunted commonness, may be representative of the community, is he our model citizen? Should we mirror our behavior in the same way that he would? The reasonable man sets the bar legally, but in doing so, does he actually lower it morally? This median personality—the average citizen playing it safe, tucked away in the middle of the pack—is not self-guided by a deep sense of moral courage and virtue. And yet this is the very person whose conduct establishes the standard for the rest of us in determining what passes for law in America.[6]

Like many victims and litigants, Rosenbaum wants justice to embody everyday moral reasoning. Frustrated by decisions based on statutes, precedents, and stylized categories, many recipients of legal justice take two steps that the legal system itself rarely takes: they blame the courts for their narrow view, and they extend their indictment to other people, even whole categories of other people. They blame the judge, the jury, the rich, the powerful, or their favorite categories of malefactors.

In the West Warwick case, survivors and relatives complained that the judge had denied them just compensation for a hundred deaths. The band manager and one owner got four years each in prison, while the second owner escaped with community service. The judge himself declared that the sentences wouldn't assuage survivors' grief. Even the younger brother said it might have been better if he had died. He made his bid to join the victims on the honorable side of an us-them boundary. In this case, the justice detector worked overtime.

THE VALUE OF DEAD CHILDREN

The Rhode Island detector produced a big negative score partly because the hundred fire victims were mostly young people just starting their careers. On the whole, the younger the victim, the greater the blame. Chapter 2 showed us a New Jersey jury awarding seven-year-old Antonia Verni more than 100 million dollars for the blight that a drunken driver had put on her life five years earlier. Antonia survived the crash, but as a paraplegic. Her injuries plunged her into a living death. In the contemporary United States, killing or maiming a child drives the justice detector to rare heights.

It was not always so. Princeton University sociologist and cultural historian Viviana Zelizer has clarified how blaming works in valuation of a child's death or serious injury.

During the nineteenth century, Zelizer shows, Americans made a crucial shift. As child employment in farms and mills diminished and children's school attendance became more general, children lost much of their immediate economic value to families. Young children became economic liabilities. Yet, ironically, parents valued them more.

As children's death rates declined and family investments in children's futures increased, families stopped treating the death of a child as just one of those unavoidable hardships that parents faced. Children went from having a (small) market value to becoming priceless. At the same time, street railways and automobiles were killing and maiming youngsters ever more frequently. "By 1910, accidents had become the leading cause of death for children ages five to fourteen."[7]

This bundle of changes produced two remarkable results. First, parents and child advocates mobilized successfully to regulate street traffic and protect children from vehicles. The separate railroad lines, overpasses, and protected crossings Americans now take for granted came into being. Second, courts changed their way of calculating appropriate compensation for a child's wrongful death. Judges and juries had long tried to compensate families for the earnings that a killed child worker would have brought the family if she or he had survived. In an 1878 railway case, the cross-examination of an employer who testified on a five-year-old's likely future earnings ran like this:

> Q. I ask you now, what do you think [this child] is worth in money? . . . you have a step-son about twelve years old: what would you consider him worth—$10,000 from five to twenty-one?
> A. Yes, I would; boys between twelve and sixteen and twenty are worth $75 or $80 a month.

Q. Is this not rather an unusual thing, and an extraordinary boy who will get it?

A. I suppose it is not ordinary.

Q. Taking $720 per annum as the best rates a boy can earn on an average for the last six years of his minority . . . it would amount to $4,370. Deduct six years' expenses at $360 per annum, making $2,160, and it leaves the net earnings $2,210.[8]

The jury agreed, awarding $2,265 for the death of the five-year-old.

A century later, American courts had entirely changed their financial tune. Instead of paying attention to the wages a child might bring in before leaving home, they shifted their attention to other elements: the sentimental loss endured by grieving parents and the financial investment parents had made in the child's future. Courts started trying to estimate the subjective emotional value, present and future, that parents had lost. Plaintiff's lawyers accordingly took to portraying both how irreplaceable a dead or badly injured child had been and how much parents had cherished them.

In the Verni case, the trial judge himself issued this instruction to the jury:

> If you find that Antonia will not live a full life due to her injuries you may increase Antonia's loss of enjoyment of life as Antonia was . . . entitled to be compensated for not being able to live her full life. In other words, when considering damages for loss of enjoyment of life you should consider the amount which Antonia's life may be shortened and you may compensate her for such losses.[9]

The defendants' attorneys later argued successfully that the jury could not legally fix compensation for shortened life expectancy. The appeals court treated the trial judge's instruction as an error. But the court did not overturn compensation for diminished quality of life. Spoiling a child's future life, and therefore the child's value to the family, called for legal blame.

"The irony, of course," notes Zelizer, "is that the irreplaceability of the child's personal qualities must be established with the purpose of converting them into their cash equivalent."[10] As the twentieth century rolled on, awards for children's wrongful deaths shot up into large sums, calculated both as compensation for grievous losses and punishment for those who caused children to die. The awards fixed blame on competent agents who bore the responsibility for destroying immense value.

What changed during the twentieth century? Not the basic process of assigning blame to malefactors. Blamers still activated the same justice detector. They closed in on an outcome: the death or injury of a child. They looked for an agent, and estimated how competent and responsible the agent had been. On that basis, they computed the amount of harm the agent had produced. But they changed their valuation of a child's life. Where nineteenth-century parents and courts had focused on the child's lost earnings, their twentieth-century counterparts fixed on two priceless pleasures: the child's own joy at living a full life, and the parents' satisfaction at raising a creative child. (Having raised four children of my own, I can testify to those pleasures.) Court awards expanded to compensate parents and maimed children for the loss of those pleasures.

Caretakers who harm children drive parental justice detectors wild. In October 2006, New York State Supreme Court justice Bonnie Wittner sentenced baby tender Noella

Allick to ten years in prison. Allick raised two children on her native Caribbean island of St. Lucia. She then came to New York City for work as a "baby nurse." Vanessa and Patrick Donohue hired her to take care of their newborn, Sarah Jane. Allick took over when Sarah Jane was five days old. The *New York Post* reported what happened then:

> By the next day, Sarah had grown lethargic. She did not eat.
>
> Vanessa remembers Allick saying, "It's OK. She's a slow eater."
>
> By the time Sarah was 2 weeks old, she was back in the hospital.
>
> "We didn't even suspect her."
>
> But Allick eventually confessed to ferociously shaking the newborn.
>
> Today, Sarah's life is dominated by physical therapy, speech and occupational therapy. A hyperbaric oxygen chamber is used to stimulate her brain. She can't tell one face from another, crawl, or eat solid food—her brain does not tell her to chew, so she might choke.[11]

The 240-pound Allick said she had shaken Sarah Jane to wake her up and feed her. Her shaking had wrecked the baby's brain.

Allick received a concurrent five-year prison sentence for shaking another infant she cared for. In that case, she broke an arm, a leg, a collarbone, and two ribs. News media took to calling her the Monster Nurse. (Professional nurses' organizations immediately began insisting that Allick was not a certified nurse.[12]) After the sentencing, Sarah's mother screamed at Allick: "You're off in 10 years. Me and Sarah are in this forever."[12] Justice Wittner echoed the Rhode Island colleague who had sentenced the Derderians for their night-club fire:

> "Nothing I can say can comfort you," she began. "I hope that by your participation in these proceedings, and being able to express yourself, it gives you some comfort."[14]

But, of course, the baby-sitter's ten years in prison would not repair the baby's injuries or somehow transfer them to their perpetrator. Courts usually fall far short of an eye for an eye, a tooth for a tooth.

Outside of court, blame for children's hardships and disabilities often divide parents. In a searching analysis of responsibility for the health of children, Carol Heimer and Lisa Staffen report their observations of parents they encountered from a base in a clinic for critically ill newborns. They describe the case of Robert, an eighteen-month-old with hydrocephalus and spina bifida. Robert's father Mike, a construction laborer, had recently returned to his ex-wife and their three children. Robert's mother Gloria lived with her three children (the older two from previous unions), her seventeen-year-old stepbrother, and the stepbrother's sixteen-year-old girlfriend.

Although Gloria bore the brunt of Robert's extensive care, to some extent each parent blamed the other for the infant's condition. When Robert re-entered the hospital with pneumonia, for example, Gloria complained that "all of his [Mike's] kids ended up with pneumonia when they got home from the hospital."[15] Gloria described herself

> as spending nearly all of her time caring for her children, though Mike reported that she frequently went out, leaving Robert and his siblings in the care of

the sixteen-year-old "aunt." Not that this was so bad, Mike hastened to add, given that the aunt was probably at least as competent and loving as Gloria. Further, he complained, Gloria had done little to get the help that Robert needs. His own employer suggested that they take Robert to the local Shriners' hospital, which they have since done, and so the child's condition may improve.[16]

As he blamed Gloria for her neglect, Mike was placing himself on the right side of an us-them boundary, including himself with the researchers Heimer and Staffen. He located Gloria on the wrong side. Even if none of our children ever had conditions as bad as hydrocephalus and spina bifida, any of us who has raised children through sickness and other trouble probably remembers moments resembling the mutual recriminations of Gloria and Mike. Responsibility for children repeatedly activates justice detectors.

Sometimes parents themselves cross the us-them boundary into destructive territory. Alexander Masters has written an extraordinary life—and death—of Stuart Shorter. Before a night train struck him down, Stuart lived mostly on the streets of Oxford, England. He also occupied jail cells, psychiatric hospital wards, and the occasional apartment, with or without girlfriends. Masters talked to Stuart for two years as his biography took painful shape. One of Masters's stories concerns the incident in Stuart's life that Stuart himself recognized as his Unmentionable Crime: holding off the police by threatening to kill his infant son.

At age 20, Stuart was living intermittently with his girlfriend Sophie, mother of his son. At a neighborhood pub, someone told Stuart that Sophie was sleeping with one of their friends. When the pub closed, the drunken Stuart walked the street for a while, went home, watched boxing on television for a few minutes, went upstairs to the bedroom, found the sleeping Sophie, started to make love, received a rebuff, and went into a rage. He fetched a kitchen knife from downstairs, and by his own report said something like "If you don't give me all the fucking money you've got, I'm gonna kill you and everyone in the fucking house."[17]

Sophie called the police. When they arrived at the house, Stuart crossed an us-them boundary that even his patient, sympathetic biographer can't condone:

> Stuart's crime is not abated by the excuses of suspected adultery, quick defeat, disturbed youth, attempted suicide, self-hatred. When the police arrived at Stuart's house, he had done something unspeakable. "I'd got the Little 'Un in me arms, and I've still got this knife with me at the time, and I've stood by the window and I've said, 'Right, if anyone comes in the fucking house, I'm gonna kill him.'"[18]

The police disarmed Stuart, beating him mercilessly all the way down the stairs, into the street, and in the van on the way to the station, "calling me a bastard, kicking me in the bollocks and in the stomach, stamping up and down on me fucking head."[s] In prison, other inmates shunned him as a child molester. They blamed him for one of the worst crimes.

BLAME ISN'T SIMPLY CREDIT UPSIDE DOWN

Blame for damage to children puts a spotlight on very general processes in the assignment of blame. Harming a child certainly places a responsible agent on the wrong side of an us-them line; even former friends shun a child batterer. But the degree of blame depends on the assessment of outcome, agency, competence, and responsibility. If observers or courts see the agent's contribution to the child's harm as slight, consider the agent to be incompetent, or treat the outcome as an accident, blame diminishes or disappears. Blamers are making judgments even more subtle than those they make when assigning credit.

Blamers' judgments do not simply reverse the procedures for awarding credit. Blaming differs from crediting in five important regards:

- First and most obviously, those who blame estimate a loss in value rather than a gain.

- Second and less obviously, blamers usually try to calculate each perpetrator's contribution closely, with allowances for action, competence, and responsibility. In giving credit, evaluators often err on the side of generosity, ignoring luck and other people's contributions to the positive outcome. As in the Academy Awards, friends and family often share the credit for an accomplishment. Not just in courtrooms but in everyday life, however, blaming involves fine calculations of contributions to some negative outcome.

- Third, although people who claim credit sometimes exaggerate their agency, competence, and responsibility for a favorable outcome, people who want to avoid blame generally try much harder to *deny* their agency, competence, and responsibility for the unfavorable outcome.

- Fourth, evaluators of losses generally demand that the perpetrator's penalty match the loss closely. In the assignment of credit, matches between rewards and gains in value often remain very rough: a certificate, a medal, or a dignitary's handshake often rewards the saving of a life. Not so for harm or loss of life. Survivors demand just penalties and compensation.

- Finally, the us-them boundary works differently in credit and blame. Although giving credit always sorts people into worthy and less worthy, it does not necessarily establish a sharp line between ins and outs. Anyone can admire the marathon's winner. Blaming people puts them on the other side of a well-defined boundary from judges, victims, and survivors. It takes rituals of contrition and absolution to bring perpetrators back across the boundary.

Blame resembles credit as an image in a funhouse mirror resembles the person standing before it.

Existing us-them boundaries sometimes bend the assignment of blame back in the other direction: we refuse to acknowledge the guilt of our own people. A forty-year-old recollection makes the point. Young and poor, my wife Louise, our (then) three children, and I had a precious chance to spend a year at Princeton University. We couldn't afford housing in high-priced downtown Princeton, New Jersey. A few miles away, we found a big, attractive, low-rent house on an acre of land with a barn and pony stall: bonanza! We signed a year's lease.

The owner, we later learned, was a well-known local character—an amiable, divorced, hard-drinking Princeton graduate who had won a Princeton wrestling letter. Let's call him Andy. We moved in while Andy's friends were still painting and making necessary repairs. But Andy didn't actually move out: he lodged himself in the barn, and came in to use the facilities when we left for the day. Meanwhile his many creditors began dunning us for money he owed them.

While I went to Europe for a short meeting, things got worse. Andy promised to leave the premises but didn't, his shady friends hung around, and the plumbing, it turned out, included such features as a kitchen sink that emptied onto the basement floor. When I called home from Paris, Louise said she couldn't stand the situation another day. I reminded her that we had signed a lease. She went to see a lawyer. The lawyer listened to her description, and agreed that we had a case for breaking the lease and recovering our deposit. He then asked the landlord's name. Louise named Andy. The lawyer replied, "I'm sorry, I can't take the case: he's my Princeton classmate." He refused to cross the us-them boundary separating Princeton classmates from everyone else. Louise got another attorney and found another house. Soon after my return from France, we moved.

The trivial Princeton episode shares properties with momentous political events. When national leaders deny that their troops could have committed genocide, when warring nations try to shift the blame for massacres to the other side, or when party leaders refuse to punish corrupt followers, us-them boundaries override the usual work of estimating competence and responsibility for some negative outcome.[20] Loyalty overcomes justice.

Justice becomes more salient and demanding in blame. This means, of course, that negative counterparts of tournaments, honors, promotions, and networks come into being. Cascades of blame replace tournaments, as whole populations of competitors condemn a cheater or sore loser. Treatments ranging from shunning to expulsion replace honors, as organizations label former members as dishonorable. Demotions and degradations replace promotions. Meanwhile, shaming displaces praise within networks, for example when a friend who has blurted out your secrets must work his way back into your confidence. The exact contents of these blaming routines vary from group to group. But they all involve stories of outcome, agency, competence, responsibility, and us-them distinctions. Once people have assigned blame, furthermore, they always call for justice.

MAKING THE PUNISHMENT FIT THE CRIME

But how can we recognize justice when we see it? The Japanese emperor has an answer. In Gilbert and Sullivan's comic operetta *The Mikado*, the emperor arrives in the town of Titipu, and almost accidentally unravels a set of plots that only G&S could have invented. As he arrives, the emperor boasts that he is a "true philanthropist." To back up his claim, he sings about how he intends "To make, to some extent / Each evil liver / A running river / of harmless merriment." How?

> My object all sublime
> I shall achieve in time—
> To let the punishment fit the crime—
> The punishment fit the crime;
> And make each prisoner pent
> Unwillingly represent
> A source of innocent merriment!
> Of innocent merriment!

Among other well-matched penalties:

> The advertising quack who wearies
> With tales of countless cures,

His teeth, I've enacted,
Shall all be extracted
By terrified amateurs.
The music-hall singer attends a series
Of masses and fugues and "ops"
By Bach, interwoven
With Spohr and Beethoven,
At classical Monday Pops.

The billiard sharp whom any one catches,
His doom's extremely hard—
He's made to dwell—
In a dungeon cell
On a spot that's always barred.
And there he plays extravagant matches
In fitless finger-stalls
On a cloth untrue,
With a twisted cue
And elliptical billiard balls!

My object all sublime, etc.[21]

The Mikado's ingenious sentences voice the principle of poetic justice. They strike listeners as amusingly right because they so neatly equate the penalty to the blame an offender ought to receive. They retaliate. The word resonates because it echoes the Latin *talio*, a punishment similar to the injury done. It probably also resonates because it follows a set of rules that evolution has wired into human brains: Do unto others as they have done to you.

The complex academic field called game theory sheds light on how tit-for-tat rules work. Students of game theory often begin their educations with the prisoner's dilemma.

The police arrest two suspects in a theft, and have enough evidence to convict them of trespassing. If each one implicates the other, they both get medium sentences for theft. But the cops can't make the charge of theft stick unless at least one implicates the other. Speaking to the two suspects separately, they make the following offer to each: implicate your partner, and we'll let you off with a suspended sentence, unless of course he implicates you; refuse to cooperate, and we'll get you convicted for trespassing.

If both refuse the cops' offer, each of them receives a conviction for trespassing. If one implicates and the other refuses, however, the snitch receives a suspended sentence while the other one gets a long jail term for theft. The police make sure that the two prisoners have no chance to consult with each other before deciding. The dilemma: refuse the offer, or blame your partner?

Most of us avoid the prisoner's dilemma in that narrow form. But we face it all the time in a more general version: If we do favors for a friend who doesn't reciprocate or even does us dirt, how should we respond? Should we blame him, delivering bad deed for bad deed? Or should we give him one more chance to prove himself?

Insiders call that more general version of the problem an iterated prisoner's dilemma. In 1979, when we were colleagues at the University of Michigan, political scientist Robert Axelrod ran two famous computer tournaments. Axelrod designed them to identify the strategy that would produce the largest long-run payoff for a single player in repeated runs of the prisoner's dilemma. He invited game theorists, computer specialists, and natural scientists to try their skills.

Some of Axelrod's contestants submitted elaborate programs. In both rounds, mathematician and peace researcher

Anatol Rapaport, from the University of Toronto, sent in the simplest program: tit for tat. Tit for tat is "merely the strategy of starting with cooperation, and thereafter doing what the other player did on the previous move."[22] In both tournament rounds, Rapaport's tit for tat won. Rip away the disguises: you'll discover that tit for tat, an eye for an eye, and the Mikado's poetic justice look pretty much the same. All of them announce contingent retaliation. They strike resonant chords in human brains.

When ordinary people look for justice, they regularly follow Anatol Rapoport's lead. At first, they commonly call for contingent retaliation. But that intuitively attractive call contradicts four competing justice principles. We can call them incapacitation, deterrence, rehabilitation, and restoration. They involve very different responses to blame. The differences run like this:

Incapacitation responds to blame by incarcerating, maiming, killing, or otherwise removing a perpetrator's capacity to repeat the offense: Lock 'em up, and throw away the key. The range runs from giving an unruly child bedroom time to mass deportation and ethnic cleansing.

Deterrence shifts attention away from particular perpetrators to send a general message to would-be malefactors: Don't do it, or you'll receive a terrible penalty. The range runs from time in the stocks to widely advertised nuclear tests.

Rehabilitation typically asks the perpetrator to show remorse and reform, but returns him or her to something like the moral situation before the offense: Prove you're sorry and have changed, then we'll take you back. The range runs from simple apologies to forced re-education.

Restoration concentrates on knitting the offended community back together, which may or may not also involve retaliation, incapacitation, deterrence, or rehabilitation: Let's grieve together before getting on with the world. The range runs from prayer meetings to truth and reconciliation commissions.

Criminologist John Hagan points out that from the 1980s onward American penal policy moved away from rehabilitation and even retaliation toward incapacitation in the name of deterrence. American authorities blamed black males for high crime rates. They therefore tried to reduce crime rates by locking up the offenders. They adopted selective incapacitation. Advocates reasoned that "withdrawing a large proportion of very active offenders from the larger population" would reduce crime dramatically.[23] As a result, the United States achieved the world's highest rates of imprisonment.

A telling comparison pits the United States against South Africa in 1990, at a time when the collapsing apartheid state had not yet emptied its jails. For the black male populations, the rates of incarceration were 3,370 per 100,000 in the United States and 681 per 100,000 in South Africa.[24] The U.S. rate of incarceration for black males ran almost exactly five times higher than the South African rate.

Most of the American prison sentences punished drug-related offenses. A double irony—or injustice—occurs: most American users of hard drugs are not black but white, and the sentences far exceed the blame most Americans assign to hard drug use.[25] Deterrence and rehabilitation look implausible as rationales for the policy. More likely some combination of incapacitation and restoration has come into play, with a tinge of retaliation: lock up the most dangerous offenders, reunite a frightened white population, and strike back at black people for the harm they have done to whites. All three reinforce the us-them boundary. But their coexistence proves that penal policy involves more than simply making the punishment fit the crime. It involves a balance among conflicting agendas, only one of which is the assignment of blame.

BLAME FOR 9/11

Take the public discussion of 9/11. It certainly produced calls for retaliation, incapacitation, deterrence, and restoration, although not much rehabilitation. American invasions of Afghanistan and Iraq combined all these rationales, with a broadly defined category of "terrorists" as the malefactors to be punished.

But who were the malefactors, and what did they do? On the morning of 11 September 2001, nineteen young Middle Eastern men separately boarded four commercial flights from Boston, Newark, and Washington Dulles. American Airlines Flight 11 was headed from Boston to Los Angeles, United Flight 175 likewise headed from Boston to Los Angeles, United Flight 93 from Newark to San Francisco, and American Flight 77 from Washington to Los Angeles.

Soon after takeoff, the nineteen men took over their flights. The hijackers diverted Flights 11 and 175 to New York, and flew them directly into the World Trade Center's twin towers at 8:46 and 9:03 AM. The hijackers on Flight 77 crashed it into the Pentagon at 9:37. On Flight 93, passengers started resisting the takeover about half an hour after it occurred. As passengers struggled with the hijackers, the aircraft crashed into a field in Shanksville, Pennsylvania, well short of its

Washington, DC destination. That crash also killed everyone on board the plane.

In the World Trade Center, about 15,000 people who worked in the towers evacuated successfully, but over 2,000 — overwhelmingly working or meeting at or above the level of the aircrafts' impact — died. In the two airplanes that struck the Trade Center, 157 people including the hijackers died. The Pentagon attack killed 64 people in the aircraft and another 125 people on the ground. The New York Fire Department lost 343 members, the Police Department 23. Altogether, nearly 3,000 people died that day in commandeered aircraft, struck buildings, or the immediate surroundings of those buildings.[26] The disaster immediately launched a national debate about credit and blame. Who should take responsibility for these terrible losses?

The suicide attacks did not just frighten Americans and draw attention to al-Qaeda's threats. They also put the U.S. government in a bind. With nearly 3,000 people dead as a result of crashes by hijacked commercial airliners, they raised the specter of immense, crippling lawsuits for culpable neglect against airlines, building owners, and public officials. They also raised questions about what sorts of preventive measures the government could and should have taken. Five years later, Internet wires still hum with conspiratorial stories of corporate and official complicity in the attacks.[27]

Soon after 9/11, Congress acted to diffuse the blame. It set up a large but manageable Victim Compensation Fund (VCF). Survivors who could prove their losses and who agreed to abstain from lawsuits became eligible for financial compensation based on those losses. Fund master Kenneth Feinberg and his staff evaluated thousands of claims. They routinely applied formulas including present and future financial losses from deaths, injuries, and property damage.

They included the commercial value of unpaid services the victims would have rendered. But they also provided uniform compensation for loss of companionship. Who deserved such compensation—surviving children, parents, siblings, spouses, lovers, and others—became intense matters of contention.[28]

By no means everyone who received compensation, furthermore, found the government's response adequate. Ron Breitweiser, a prosperous money manager for Fiduciary Trust, died in the attack on the World Trade Center's south tower. His wife Kristen, a lawyer who was not currently practicing law, survived across the Hudson River in New Jersey with their two-year-old daughter Caroline. Kristen Breitweiser became a pivotal figure in American political struggles over 9/11. She subtitled her later book on the subject *The Political Education of a 9/11 Widow*. Immediately after 9/11, Breitweiser tells us there, she nearly went mad with grief.

Two months after 9/11, a November 2001 meeting with lawyers about the proposed VCF switched Breitweiser onto a political track. She was soon attending meetings, speaking for survivors' rights. She began working closely with three other World Trade Center widows from New Jersey: Patty Casazza, Mindy Kleinberg, and Lorie Van Auken. The four of them became scourges of evasive politicians:

> We were devastated by the loss of our husbands, but we were fueled by our anger and fear, and our belief that our husbands did not have to die. We understood that there was a difference between victims and survivors. Our husbands had become senseless victims. We were going to be survivors. Bin Laden had murdered 3,000 victims, four of whom were our husbands. We were not going to rest until we knew that something like 9/11 would never happen again.[29]

That quest led them into repeated struggles to assign blame for 9/11.

It also started a series of challenges to the government's handling of the subsequent crisis. Breitweiser writes with bitterness about the Victims' Compensation Fund. She portrays it as political cover for a Congress that handed the airlines $15 billion for their losses and denied the survivors of wealthier victims (including her husband Ron) the right to sue for maintenance of their pre-9/11 standard of living.[30] She complains that trial lawyers eagerly took up suits against the airlines on behalf of passengers who died in the four crashes of 9/11, but encouraged ground victims to join the VCF.[31] She and her allies also began raising pointed questions about the government's failure to prevent the attacks despite extensive information about bin Laden's plans and about the hijackers themselves.[32] They demanded accountability—the assignment of blame.

Over strong resistance from President George W. Bush and (especially) Vice President Richard Cheney, the New Jersey widows lobbied successfully for an independent commission to investigate the 9/11 disaster. Senators Joe Lieberman, John McCain, and Robert Torricelli first proposed the commission's formation to the Senate in October 2001.[33] It would probably would have gone nowhere without outside pressure, including pressure from 9/11 families.

The White House first resisted any commission at all, then insisted on naming its chair and denying the commission any subpoena power. It finally conceded the subpoena power as well as the appointment of a vice chair and half the other commissioners by the congressional Democratic leadership. The president named the ever-present presidential adviser Henry Kissinger as chair.

One of Breitweiser's most compelling stories describes a meeting at Kissinger's Washington offices. The widows demanded that Kissinger provide a list of his clients they could check for possible conflicts of interest. Kissinger said he would release the list to an attorney agreed upon by the 9/11 families and himself. The other widows identified Breitweiser as an attorney. A flustered Kissinger backed off. The next day he resigned as commission chair.[34] Soon after, vice chairman and former senator George Mitchell also resigned.

The widows finally got their commission. It now included former New Jersey governor Thomas Kean as (Republican) chair and former congressman Lee Hamilton as (Democratic) vice chair. Presidential advisers Karl Rove and Andrew Card recruited Kean, while Democratic leader Tom Daschle persuaded Hamilton, already a commission member, to co-chair it.[35] In March 2003, the National Commission on Terrorist Attacks Upon the United States held its first public hearing at the Alexander Hamilton U.S. Customs House in Manhattan, not far from the leveled site of the World Trade Center.

At that hearing, Breitweiser's fellow widow Mindy Kleinberg made a statement representing the widows' collective view. She attacked the government's theory that the hijackers had simply benefited from good luck:

> With regard to the 9/11 attacks, it has been said that the intelligence agencies have to be right 100% of the time and the terrorists only have to get lucky once. This explanation for the devastating attacks of September 11th, simple on its face, is wrong in its value. Because the 9/11 terrorists were not just lucky once: they were lucky over and over again.[36]

Kleinberg went on to enumerate a number of intelligence botches and anomalies. She mentioned, among other major slips, the visas issued to the nineteen hijackers, their smuggling of contraband weapons onto the aircraft, and military failure to intercept the hijacked jets.

Other witnesses joined the widows in raising doubts whether responsible government agencies and officials had properly defended the country against terrorists. At hearings, audiences often joined in with applause or signs of dissent. When Rudy Giuliani, New York mayor at the time of 9/11, testified before the commission, a wild scene ensued:

> As the questioning period went on, some families in the audience became audibly upset. Near the end of the session [commission member] Slade Gorton detailed the successes of the rescue operation, asking, "Would it be accurate to say that your people saved, at this cost of 403 of their own lives, 99.5 percent or more of the people they could conceivably have saved?" In his answer, Giuliani said that firefighters who had received an evacuation order chose to stay and save lives. At this point, the audience erupted into shouting. Some yelled, "Talk about the radios!" or "Put one of us on the panel!" or "My son was murdered because of your incompetence!" Others started trying to shout them down; many people were standing.[37]

Despite the widows' incessant pressure, the commission mostly failed to name names and fix responsibility. Prominent defenders of the Bush administration portrayed it as a witch hunt.

Both Attorney General John Ashcroft and House Judiciary Committee chair James Sensenbrenner, for example, attacked commissioner Jamie Gorelick (the only woman on the ten-person commission) as a Clintonite. She had served as deputy attorney general in the Clinton administration.[38]

The commission got into major political flaps over the testimony of Secretary of State Condoleezza Rice, Rice's former security deputy Richard Clarke, Defense Secretary Donald Rumsfeld, Vice President Cheney, and President Bush himself. On the whole, administration supporters accused the commission of undermining the war on terror.

The widows, in contrast, came to see the investigations and hearings as a whitewash. They identified commission executive director Philip Zelikow (later State Department counselor) as the administration's stalking horse. The commission's 567-page report, prepared under Zelikow's close supervision, appeared in July 2004.[39] It provided a dramatic narrative of the hijackers' preparations and the 9/11 events. As a student of terrorism, I found the account of al-Qaeda's involvement in the attacks surprisingly well done for an official document.[40]

That wasn't the problem. The commission's report faulted the intelligence community for failing, especially in the CIA's refusal to hand over crucial information to the FBI. It called for an overhaul of the American intelligence system. But it declined to assign blame to specific individuals, organizations, or national administrations. The commission's bipartisan composition, its direction by a sometime administration official, and a final review by the White House itself apparently kept it from fixing blame inside the U.S. government.

The widows found the report disappointing. They wanted blame. They weren't alone. Influential critic Benjamin De-Mott concluded that

> The plain, sad reality—I report this following four full days studying the work—is that *The 9/11 Commission Report*, despite the vast quantity of labor behind it, is a cheat and a fraud. It stands as a series of evasive

maneuvers that infantilize the audience, transform candor into iniquity, and conceal realities that demand immediate inspection of confrontation . . . In the course of blaming everybody a little, the Commission blames nobody—blurs the reasons for the actions and hesitations of successive administrations, masks choices that, fearlessly defined, might actually have vitalized our public political discourse.[41]

The 9/11 families, DeMott, and many other critics were calling for the identification of an us-them boundary with responsible governmental officials on one side and victims on the other.

Unsurprisingly, commission co-chairs Kean and Hamilton denied that person by person, blame would have been possible or just:

We did not think this kind of approach would be helpful. First, 9/11 was not the fault of any one individual. Singling out individuals—saying Joe Smith or Mary Johnson failed in their duty—and thus assigning culpability for the deaths of nearly 3,000 Americans, would have drawn a disproportionate amount of attention. The story of 9/11 is not a story of how a handful of government employees made mistakes; it is the story of how an entire government—across two administrations and many bureaucracies—failed to understand and adjust to the growing threat from al Qaeda, and was poorly organized to combat terrorism. We could not draw a straight line of causation from a mistake or decision by one official to the events of 9/11; this event was much too complex for that kind of analysis.[42]

The co-chairs refused to play the blame game.

What's more, the Bush administration reacted by saying only that it would study the report, not that it would adopt the report's recommendations. The administration's non-response helped persuade the New Jersey widows to campaign for Democrats John Kerry and John Edwards in the 2004 presidential election. Failure of the Kerry-Edwards ticket scuttled their hopes of seeing the report's modest recommendations implemented seriously.

With many other Americans who found 9/11 appalling, the New Jersey widows were not merely seeking to prevent another disaster. They were trying to get public institutions to fix blame. They had a clear outcome in mind: the attacks of 9/11/2001. The commission amply documented the involvement of al-Qaeda operatives in that outcome. The widows, however, wanted assignment of competence and responsibility for that outcome going beyond al-Qaeda coordination. They asked which American agencies and officials had failed. They called for punishment to match the crime, and for a clearer boundary between those who did and did not deserve blame. Failing to receive that justice, they cried out in righteous indignation.

Blame occurs in public debate, in courts, and in everyday life. Although the word "justice" alone often calls up a warm glow, justice commonly consists first of fixing blame, then of imposing penalties for blame. More so than the giving of credit, assigning blame can easily become a persistent, destructive habit. Many a friendship, partnership, or marriage breaks up over the assignment of blame. But when carried out successfully through retaliation, incapacitation, deterrence, rehabilitation, and/or restoration, blaming brings struggles to an end. We should salute just blame's creative destruction.

5 | MEMORIES OF VICTORY, LOSS, AND BLAME

My brother Richard has become more or less German. Despite his growing up in Illinois, his nearly fifty years of analyzing German history and nearly forty years of living in Germany have left him with a German family, a German accent, and a German perspective on world affairs. Meanwhile, my family was becoming French, although not to the extent that Richard's was becoming German. My son Chris was born in Angers, France. All of us eventually accumulated years of French residence. When Richard's and my families get together, we often compare notes on French-German-American differences.

A few years after Richard and his charming Würzburg-born wife Elisabeth moved from New Haven, Connecticut back to Germany, my family visited them from France. During the visit, the two families went on an excursion I never forgot. In the thick Teutoburg Forest near Detmold, we joined hundreds of Germans who were picnicking at the Hermann Monument. Two million people per year visit the monument, the most popular in all Germany.

"Hermann" mistranslates Armin, a Germanic warrior and sometime Roman ally. In 9 A.D., Armin defeated three Roman legions under Publius Quinctilius Varus in the Teutoburg

Forest. In his *Annals,* Roman historian Tacitus described the former Roman ally as the rival of German leader Segestes, who remained loyal to Rome:

> But Varus fell by fate and by the sword of Arminius, with whom Segestes, though dragged into war by the unanimous voice of the nation, continued to be at feud, his resentment being heightened by personal motives, as Arminius had carried off his daughter who was betrothed to another.[1]

For Romans, read French: during the nineteenth century, Armin became a national symbol of resistance to the French forces that had invaded and conquered much of Germany during the Napoleonic Wars. Sculptor Ernst von Bandel started building the patriotic monument in 1838. But he didn't finish the job until 1875. By then, Prussia had trounced France in the Franco-Prussian War of 1870–1871, Napoleon III's Second Empire had collapsed, Prussia had taken Alsace and much of Lorraine from France as spoils of war, and Germany had united under Prussian leadership.

With its base, Armin's commanding statue reaches 175 feet above the ground. The huge sword in Armin's right hand points toward France, and bears the inscription "Germany's unity is my strength, my strength is Germany's might." We tourists couldn't see the inscription, however. Although the huge statue contains a hollow interior with a steep stairway reaching to the statue's head and arms, tourists can't get past the 69 steps that lead up to its feet. But we did see the monument's cornerstone, with its message calculated to chill Francophiles:

> To Arminius. Thou once drove Rome's legions beyond the Rhine, and Germans now thank thee for Germany's

existence. If France's plundering hordes greedily threaten the homeland's Rhenish lands, swing thy sword again.[2]

Credit and blame join forcefully in these vividly vindictive words. In 1875, united Germans took credit for humiliating presumptuous France. They retaliated monumentally for decades of French scorn.

The French took a while to reply. In 1867, as Garibaldi led the drive for Italian unification, Emperor Napoleon III's troops had defended the pope from Garibaldi's forces. But in 1870, war-torn France withdrew its soldiers, and Italian patriots seized the Papal States. Then German troops humiliated French armies and took the French emperor prisoner. How could the French restore their national honor? Immediately after the disastrous Franco-Prussian War, French Catholics proposed to wash away national sin and shame by two measures: a campaign to organize popular devotions around the Sacred Heart of Jesus, and construction of a Parisian church dedicated to those devotions. Reasonably, they called the hoped-for church Sacré Coeur: Sacred Heart.

The plan's originator, Alexander Legentil, fled Paris as Prussian armies approached. In the provinces, he swore that "if God saved Paris and France and delivered the sovereign pontiff, he would contribute according to his means to the construction in Paris of a sanctuary dedicated to the Sacred Heart."[3] In 1873, a very Catholic National Assembly authorized the church's construction on the city's highest hill, Montmartre—the Martyrs' Mountain, in one disputed etymology. It took another decade to raise the funds, clear the site, and lay the foundation.

Montmartre already had a religious history. Popular legend made it the site of martyrdom for the first bishop of Paris, St. Denis, at the end of the third century. As for the Sacred

Heart of Jesus, its veneration had originated during the seventeenth century, under King Louis XIV. In 1864, Pope Pius IX beatified the cult's seventeenth-century founder, Marguerite-Marie Alacoque. By 1873, she and it had become favorites of monarchist, anti-revolutionary Catholics. The combination of the Sacred Heart with Montmartre therefore had powerful resonance in the France of the 1870s.

Montmartre also acquired anti-religious significance as the starting point of the 1871 Paris Commune. The Commune began in March when the defeated government ordered troops to remove cannons from Montmartre's heights, where they had served the ineffectual defense against the German army. Parisian workers resisted the move, and the soldiers on guard refused to fire on them. Members of the crowd later seized and killed generals Lecomte and Thomas near the hill—Lecomte had ordered the troops to fire, and Thomas had commanded troops who slaughtered workers during the Revolution of 1848. As national troops massacred communards in May 1871, furthermore, a vengeful detachment of communards murdered the archbishop of Paris. On Montmartre's heights, the secular image of the Commune confronted the religious image of the Sacred Heart. Despite fierce secular and Republican opposition, the Sacred Heart project won.

The new archbishop of Paris took responsibility for the project in January 1872. He wrote to Legentil:

> You have considered from their true perspectives the ills of our country . . . The conspiracy against God and Christ has prevailed in a multitude of hearts and in punishment for an almost universal apostasy, society has been subjected to all the horrors of war with a victorious foreigner and an even more horrible war amongst

the children of the same country. Having become, by our prevarication, rebels against heaven, we have fallen during our troubles into the abyss of anarchy. The land of France presents the terrifying image of a place where no order prevails, while the future offers still more terrors to come . . . This temple, erected as a public act of contrition and reparation . . . will stand amongst us as a protest against other monuments and works of art erected for the glorification of vice and impiety.[4]

The archbishop got his basilica. He got it located on Paris's highest hill.

Sacré Coeur started going up in 1875, the same year that Germans finished building the Hermann Monument. Construction of the striking white travertine building ended in 1914, just in time for World War I. In contrast to the French humiliation of 1870, Germany lost that war. After Germany's painful defeat, Sacré Coeur, like the Hermann Monument, became a favorite tourist destination. If you have visited Paris, you have most likely stopped at Sacré Coeur. In case anyone should miss the church's national significance, equestrian statues of Joan of Arc and Saint Louis recall France's military destiny.

In his 1898 novel *Paris*, secular republican Emile Zola called Sacré Coeur a "citadel of the absurd."[5] Eugène Ogé drew one of the era's best-known anticlerical posters as an advertisement for the republican newspaper *La Lanterne*. It showed an immense, devilish priest wrapped around Sacré Coeur and blotting out the rest of Paris. The poster's motto: *Voilà l'ennemi*—here's the enemy![6] For believers, however, Sacré Coeur came to represent the confrontation of credit and blame: credit for sustaining faith, blame for sins that weakened France.

Just about everyone remembers some humiliation for which it would be gratifying to get back at the perpetrators. We all carry at least a chip or two on our shoulders. Yet few of us build monuments to credit or blame. We leave that sort of work to priests, poets, and politicians. Some of their monuments go up stone by stone, like the Hermann Monument and Sacré Coeur. Others consist of widely shared stories, symbols, or artistic representations. This chapter examines how credit and blame's monument builders do their work. Their work constructs collective memory.

As we approach memories of victory, loss, and blame, we enter rough ground. Our individual memories are bad enough: selective, self-serving, and sometimes invented.[7] Collective memory complicates things. Every collective memory emerges from a contest among advocates of competing accounts concerning what happened and why.[8] Every monument to the past advances some interpretations of its meaning and suppresses others. The monumental statue of Armin suppresses the fact that he served for years as a Roman ally who spread the use of Latin among Germans. The white domes of Sacré Coeur make no reference to the deep divisions within France dug by the Franco-Prussian War, the Commune, and the basilica's very construction.

Struggles over collective memory pivot on credit and blame. Both, as usual, involve identification of outcomes, competence, responsibility, and us-them boundaries. Advocates struggle over each element. On the credit side, competition concerns which outcome added how much value, who had the competence to produce that outcome, to what extent they did so deliberately with knowledge of the likely consequences, and who else deserves to receive the credit, if only because of shared commitment to the cause. France's Catholic royalists congratulated themselves for maintaining a faithful remnant in the face of national adversity and perversity.

On the blame side, competition concerns which outcome damaged some valued activity, and by how much. It also concerns who had the competence and deliberated intention to produce the damage, and who else should share the blame, if only through guilt by association. Blame took up more space than credit in French national discussions of the Franco-Prussian War and the Commune. Two competing assignments of blame confronted each other:

- On one side, Catholic royalists lumped together the defeated empire, republicans, communards, and secularists on the wrong side of the us-them boundary.

- On the other, secular republicans blamed the remnants of a corrupt empire and their ecclesiastical hangers-on.

The two accounts agreed on the outcome that needed explaining: the political collapse of 1870–1871. But judgments of competence, responsibility, and value lost came close to mirror opposites. According to Catholic monarchists, secular republicans had almost destroyed France with their knowing, effective rejection of sacred traditions. According to secular republicans, the Second Empire's imperial gestures, corruption, and compromises with the Church had undermined national commitments to muscular democracy. In general, of course, collective credit and blame interact much of the time: we take the credit for saving a situation that our enemies had made toxic. The justice detector's two sides influence each other.

MEMORIES OF WAR

War stimulates collective attributions of credit and blame more often than any other human activity. Even revolutions, bungled natural disasters, political corruption, and economic crises produce less collective pointing of fingers at villains and heroes. Wars begin, after all, with built-in divisions between us and them. They continue with losses of life and property that some people always think unjustified. Won, lost, or stalemated, they end with participants making collective claims about who gets the credit and who's to blame. A costly but unsuccessful war such as the French and American adventures in Vietnam compounds the problem of assigning credit and blame; now we have to deal not only with the military enemy, but with who got us into the mess, and how.

War memorials continue the argument past the peace treaties. Despite most visibly awarding credit, war memorials always display the interaction of credit and blame. In their own distinctive ways, both the Hermann Monument and Sacré Coeur serve as war memorials. Behind the glorification of German warriors we detect the vilification of France. Behind the sanctification of the French faithful we detect the condemnation of secularists, republicans, radicals, and German invaders. A stark us-them boundary marks the difference.

Across the western world, when communities and countries pool their efforts to build symbolic structures, they most often erect churches, war memorials, or both at once. Valley Forge National Park, for example, commemorates George Washington's legendary 1777 winter encampment in preparation for engagement with British forces near Philadelphia. Its Washington Memorial Chapel features carvings that represent Washington's brigades, flags for the Army, Navy, and

French forces, seals from the 50 states, pews dedicated to different patriots, a window portraying periods of Washington's life, and a tablet over the door with the Declaration of Independence. Beside the door tourists see

> a statue of Washington showing " . . . him bearing the burdens of war — anxiety in his face, determination in the grip of the sword, confidence and hope in the pose of the entire figure." The chapel is easily interpreted as a political expression of the concept of God and country. The architectural message is that the United States was the righteous result of obeying God's will under the leadership of George Washington.[9]

Despite enormous architectural differences, Parisian tourists who visit Valley Forge can recognize surprising similarities with the symbolism of Sacré Coeur. God defends our national cause, as the ungodly undermine it. On one side of the us-them boundary stand Washington, his soldiers, their allies, and patriots in general. On the other squirm America's enemies. In 1777, of course, those enemies included Great Britain. Enemies change, but the us-them boundary remains.

Even when they don't incorporate chapels or churches, war memorials breathe sacredness.[10] Corrupt them with commercial, secular, or unpatriotic themes at your peril! But they also become sites of struggle over the proper interpretation of patriotism. Controversies over the Vietnam Veterans Memorial of Washington, DC resembled those that later roiled both the 9/11 commission and decisions about rebuilding the site of the World Trade Center's twin towers, Ground Zero. Vietnam veterans took the initiative in pressing for a memorial. Once Congress authorized the two-acre site, however, a committee without a single veteran ran the competition. Yale architecture student Maya Lin won the competition with a v-shaped granite structure containing the names of all the military dead in order of reported death. It eventually became one of the most visited and admired memorial sites in Washington.

Yet it began in controversy. At the start, organized veterans complained bitterly about the abstract design. Many said that by failing to represent heroism directly it perpetuated the picture of Vietnam veterans as losers. They prevailed. They got a second memorial 120 feet away from the first. It included a flagpole and a sculpture of three GIs looking grimly determined. At the dedication of the double monument, nevertheless, plenty of veterans renewed their complaints:

> This country sucks as far as the Vietnam Memorial helping out. We're how many years into this before we even get recognized.
>
> Came here to honor those guys living *and* dead. That's what I came here for.
>
> I got mixed emotions. The monument. The only reason I'm here is that there're three names on it. I was to see if they're on there, that's all.[11]

People did come by the thousands to trace names of the fallen. The wall contained almost 60,000 names of dead and missing military personnel. Visitors were simultaneously assigning credit and blame for those lost warriors.

The day will surely come when Americans decide collectively how to commemorate the twenty-first-century U.S. interventions in Afghanistan and Iraq. Already Americans are struggling over the meanings of those wars. Sometimes they are making explicit connections with earlier wars. When the U.S. campaign in Iraq began touching Homer, Alaska, both supporters and opponents of the war began demonstrating near the small city's war memorial. Although nearby Anchor Point displayed nothing but pro-war symbols, Homer divided:

> While those showing their support for the U.S.-led war in Iraq have Anchor Point all to themselves on Saturdays, they have only begun joining the peace activists on the corner at Pioneer and Lake for the past several weeks. For weeks prior to that, passers-by out around noon on a Monday would see a subdued silent vigil taking place on the corner, which is also the site of Homer's Veteran's Memorial. The presence of protestors in front of the memorial stirred up resentment among some residents, prompting a call to begin a counter rally at the same time. "We want to take the corner back," said one flag-waving demonstrator. "Why don't you pray for our troops instead of for the Iraqis?" yelled a passing motorist, responding to the Women in Black assertion that their vigil is in observance of those lost in war.
>
> But Sharon Whytal said she believed the choice to stand near the Veteran's Memorial symbolizes a concern for all those who are lost in military conflict. "It's true that many of us are there because we're grieving for the loss of veterans," Whytal said, adding that having both groups share the site also provides a powerful symbol—freedom in action.
>
> While there had been reports of some unpleasant exchanges between the two groups, there was little sign of it on Monday as close to 100 people stood on the

corner, split evenly. The group waving flags stood out front on the sidewalk, lined up at the curb waving flags and cheering as passing motorists honked and waved. Standing 15 yards behind them, a line of Women in Black joined by a number of men, also dressed in black, remained silent for the duration of their vigil. "I don't feel offended that there are two groups there expressing their minds," Whytal said, referring to a sign bearing a slogan popular at many protests around the country: "This is what democracy looks like."[12]

Homerites had reached a compromise. As at the Hermann Memorial, Sacré Coeur, and Valley Forge, they could treat memorials simultaneously as sites of veneration and of communication. But such compromises only work within limits. Imagine what would have happened if the Women in Black had sloshed blood, or red paint, on the nearby war memorial. Just don't desecrate these sacred spaces!

Not that Americans who differ on the Iraq War always end up in sweet harmony. In the affluent San Francisco suburb of Lafayette, building contractor Jeff Heaton created a hillside memorial to the war's American dead. He got his inspiration, he said, from a visit to Washington's Vietnam War Memorial. Heaton's homemade memorial contained 450 white wooden crosses and a 5-by-16-foot sign reading "In memory of 2,867 U.S. Troops Killed in Iraq." While the war continued, stressing the number of war deaths smacked of subversion. Former Marine sergeant Jean Bonadio objected strenuously. Driving by the hillside, she stopped her car and tore down the sign. "My first reaction was, 'What a disgrace to those who have sacrificed,' said Ms. Bonadio, 53, a dog trainer. "I had no tools with me, so I removed it with my bare hands and feet."[13]

A nationwide organization called Veterans for Peace sponsors similar displays elsewhere in the United States:

> Michael T. McPhearson, executive director of Veterans for Peace, which also has fields of crosses planted in four other cities, admitted that the displays sometimes provoked angry reactions. "They say we're not supporting the troops, and they say we shouldn't be doing these vigils," said Mr. McPhearson, 42, who served in the first gulf war. "But we feel that especially because we're veterans and we've served, we have the right."[14]

As a veteran of a much earlier and half-forgotten war—the Korean War of 1950 to 1953—I too feel that I earned the right to speak against the Iraq War. In so doing, of course, I join the very process I have been describing: the drawing of us-them boundaries. In Homer, Lafayette, and elsewhere, the Iraq War set in motion struggles over the true boundary between patriots and subversives.

RANKING PRESIDENTS

Wars leave far more than monuments behind them. They leave reputations of presidents in glory or in tatters. If wars end successfully under their administrations, that fact uniformly raises their reputations. If they preside over botched wars or fail to prevent disastrous wars, that fact usually depresses their reputations. Consider results from a 2000 poll of 78 scholars conducted jointly by the conservative *Wall Street Journal* and even more conservative Federalist Society. Law professor James Lindgren of Northwestern University surveyed a politically balanced sample of scholars from law, history, and political science.[15] Box 5.1 shows the scholars' average ranking of presidents before the second George Bush.

BOX 5.1
Scholars' Ranking of U.S. Presidents, 2000

GREAT
1. George Washington
2. Abraham Lincoln
3. Franklin Roosevelt

NEAR GREAT
4. Thomas Jefferson
5. Theodore Roosevelt
6. Andrew Jackson
7. Harry Truman
8. Ronald Reagan
9. Dwight Eisenhower
10. James Polk
11. Woodrow Wilson

ABOVE AVERAGE
12. Grover Cleveland
13. John Adams
14. William McKinley
15. James Madison
16. James Monroe
17. Lyndon Johnson
18. John Kennedy

AVERAGE
19. William Taft
20. John Quincy Adams
21. George H.W. Bush
22. Rutherford Hayes
23. Martin Van Buren

24. William Clinton
25. Calvin Coolidge
26. Chester Arthur

BELOW AVERAGE
27. Benjamin Harrison
28. Gerald Ford
29. Herbert Hoover
30. Jimmy Carter
31. Zachary Taylor
32. Ulysses Grant
33. Richard Nixon
34. John Tyler
35. Millard Fillmore

FAILURE
36. Andrew Johnson
37. Franklin Pierce
38. Warren Harding
39. James Buchanan

War made a difference. The three presidents who received "great" ratings—Washington, Lincoln, and Franklin Roosevelt—all led the United States during costly but finally victorious wars. The "failures" served in peacetime, although Franklin Pierce and James Buchanan received scholars' blame for failing to prevent the Civil War, while Andrew Johnson took the rap for botched reconstruction after the Civil War. Only the corrupt peacetime administration of Warren Harding lacks the taint of failure in war. Even there scholars mark down Harding for the administration's isolationism and its rejection of the League of Nations.

Poor Harding! His reputation fell quickly. At his death in office (1923), many Americans thought they had lost a great leader:

> As the Harding funeral train returned to Washington, where he was to lie in state, millions lined the route. "Ordinary Americans became suddenly aware— although they would soon forget—how much they loved their white-haired President . . . Never since Lincoln's death had there been such a quick, spontaneous outpouring of public sorrow." Whether or not the grief, magnified by radio reports, was greater than that at the deaths of Garfield and McKinley, the dismay of Americans was profound. Both supporters and foes were quick with encomiums. Harding's personal secretary George Christian described the bipartisan mood by noting, "I have lost the best friend I ever had, and so has every American." Harry Daugherty described Harding as a "modern Abraham Lincoln."[16]

Later, Americans came to blame Harding for cronyism, for scandals in office, for adultery in the White House;

some also accused him of concealing his African-American ancestry.

Sociologist Gary Alan Fine argues, however, that Harding's reputation, compared to that of other presidents, suffered less from his actual incompetence or corruption than from the fact that after his sudden death influential opinion-makers mostly turned against him.[17] During the decades after Lincoln's death, after all, it took a determined entrepreneurial effort to establish Lincoln as a national hero.[18] Although history came to judge Harding as relatively incompetent, it condemned him especially for degrading a great public office. After the fact, Harding's justice detector worked overtime.

Modern presidents strive to secure their historical reputations. They encourage journalists and historians to write favorable accounts, collaborate in the building of presidential libraries to house their papers, and engage in post-presidential activities that will confirm them as statesmen. George W. Bush therefore has his post-presidential work cut out for him. During his press conference of 21 December 2006, the president asked critical historians to hold off for a while:

> "Look, everybody's trying to write the history of this administration even before it's over," Bush said. "I'm reading about George Washington still. My attitude is if they're still analyzing No. 1, [No.] 43 ought not to worry about it, and just do what he thinks is right, and make the tough choices necessary."[19]

It won't be easy for No. 43's reputation to recover. Another survey underlines Bush's challenge. In 2006, Quinnipiac University pollsters asked a representative national sample of 1,534 registered voters to name the worst U.S. president since 1945:

> Strong Democratic sentiment pushes President George W. Bush to the top of the list when American voters pick the worst U.S. President in the last 61 years. Bush is named by 34 percent of voters, followed by Richard Nixon at 17 percent and Bill Clinton at 16 percent, according to a Quinnipiac University National poll released today [1 June]. Leading the list for best President since 1945 is Ronald Reagan with 28 percent, and Clinton with 25 percent.[20]

Richard Nixon's low rating comes as no surprise. Nixon bears the taints of Watergate, Vietnam, and resignation of his vice president Spiro Agnew in the shadow of a corruption scandal. The only surprise is how little opinions of Nixon vary by category of voter, including party affiliation. He counts as second worst across the board. In contrast, voters in the 2006 poll differed sharply on Jimmy Carter and Bill Clinton. Their ratings varied according to the voter's gender, religious affiliation, party affiliation, and age. At the extreme, 34 percent of Republicans and only 2 percent of Democrats identified Clinton as worst president.[21] As a result, Clinton ranked near the tops of both the "best" and "worst" lists.

In 2006, no category of voters identified by Quinnipiac pollsters rated Bush Jr. the best president since 1945. Still, different categories of voters disagreed. For example, 7 percent of self-described Republicans called Bush Jr. the worst president, as against 56 percent of self-described Democrats; 42 percent of voters aged 18–29 put Bush at the list's bottom, as compared with about 32 percent of older voters.[22]

In fact, disillusion with Bush took on an international dimension. The *Economist* magazine long supported Bush's neoliberal policies and his Iraq war. By the end of 2006, however, even the *Economist* was taking a pessimistic line on the president's prospects:

> Yet what has he to show for the blood, treasure and political capital he has spent? Not only has the world turned out to be a little more complicated than Mr. Bush presumed; his administration has hitherto proved woefully incompetent at executing his dreams. As a result, Mr. Bush's prospects in 2007 look, at first sight, pretty glum. Having deservedly lost the Republicans' grip on Congress, the president would seem to have given up the chance of any big domestic initiative. Abroad, things look even grimmer, with American troops bogged down in Iraq and Afghanistan and the unappetising issues of North Korea and Iran to deal with.[23]

At that point, the president had two years left to recoup. Bush will have to recover a great deal of ground in order to exit with a good historical reputation.

Nixon never did recover. Perhaps his resignation from the presidency in the face of certain Senate impeachment (1974) sealed Nixon's historical fate. But his presiding over the end of a disastrous war in Vietnam most likely compounded the blame. The 1967 Pentagon Papers of Robert McNamara also helped. Leaked to the *New York Times* by Daniel Ellsberg during Nixon's administration in 1971, they provided damaging material for Nixon's reputation. McNamara's papers ended their review of American policy in 1967, before Nixon took office in 1969. Four years later, nevertheless, the *Times* argued that Nixon had continued the failed policies of the Truman, Kennedy, and Johnson administrations.

The newspaper read the Pentagon Papers as an indictment of the Truman, Kennedy, Johnson, and Nixon regimes alike. The papers, according to the *Times*, documented the successive governments' ignorance, incompetence, and duplicity in the face of failure. The editors summed up their judgment:

> That these four succeeding administrations built up the American political, military and psychological stakes in Indochina, often more deeply than they realized at the time, with large-scale shipments of military equipment to the French in 1950; with acts of sabotage and terror warfare against North Vietnam beginning in 1954; with moves that encouraged and abetted the overthrow of President Ngo Dinh Diem of South Vietnam in 1963; with plans, pledges and threats of further action that sprang to life in the Tonkin Gulf clashes in August 1964; with the careful preparation of opinion for the years of open warfare that were to follow; and with the calculation in 1965, as the planes and troops were openly committed to sustained combat, that neither accommodation inside South Vietnam nor early negotiations with North Vietnam would achieve the desired result.[24]

Along with biographers, political historians, and other journalists, the *Times*'s editors were shaping historical memory. They were shaping available memories of the Vietnam War and Robert McNamara as well as of Richard Nixon.

Notice, however, what is happening to presidential reputations. By now, available memories of Washington, Lincoln, and FDR have reached a kind of equilibrium. Biographers continue to retouch their portraits. They sometimes succeed in boosting or depressing the retrospective ranking of one president or another. But generations of monuments, textbooks, popular histories, patriotic speeches, and print images have consolidated shared understandings of great presidents. The next revision won't change their images or rankings very much.

For the postwar period, consolidation hasn't yet occurred. Intellectual impresarios such as the late Arthur Schlesinger Jr. continue to revise images of such presidents as John F. Kennedy. JFK currently stands near the middle of the pack, according to the *Wall Street Journal*'s expert raters.[25] The Quinnipiac poll results suggest that Nixon's position may now be stabilizing. But wide divisions on Clinton and Bush forecast plenty of further negotiation over historical memories of their presidencies. If you want to revise American collective memory, forget about George Washington and Abraham Lincoln. Work instead on images of Bill Clinton, George W. Bush, or both together.

LATIN WAR LEADERS

Anglo-Americans are not peculiar in remembering wars, military leaders, and presidents. In fact, when it comes to monuments, holidays, street names, postage stamps, and pictures on currency, military figures occupy even more public memory space in Latin America than in the United States. Sociologist-historian Miguel Centeno has cataloged all such commemorations across Latin America. In Paraguay, Bolivia, and Peru he finds war in a majority of them.[26] For all its civil wars and military regimes, however, Latin America has engaged in far fewer interstate wars than North America and

Europe. As a result, the wars of independence from Spain (1808–1820) occupy more memory than any other struggles:

> The wars of independence stand out in the generally pacific history of Latin America. They represent a moment of martial glory, producing legends of heroism, sacrifice, and loyalty. They were the high point of Creole patriotism: the rise of a consciously American population challenging an easily identifiable enemy.[27]

Province names, national flags, and national anthems all join other monuments to the military makers of independent Latin America. Above all, Simón Bolívar, hero of Latin American independence, dominates collective memories.[28]

Born to an aristocratic family in Caracas, Venezuela (1783), Bolívar spent most of his time between 1799 and 1807 in Europe. He then returned to political life in Venezuela. Starting in 1811, he led the military campaign for independence from Spain in northern South America. It took a while. Tracked by royal and loyalist forces, Bolívar fled Venezuela for Nueva Granada (later Colombia). He returned to conquer Venezuela in 1813, but exiled himself to Jamaica in 1815. Coming back in 1817, he assembled new military forces and greater popular support. By 1819, he had become dictator of a permanently independent Gran Colombia including Venezuela and Colombia. In 1821, Gran Colombia annexed Ecuador as well. Soon Bolívar's troops and allies had also liberated a reluctant Peru. The newly liberated regime soon split into Peru and a separate country named for the liberator: Bolivia.

Within a few years, however, political rivalries undermined Bolívar's prestige and influence. Instead of giving him credit for national liberation, his rivals and successors blamed him for the arbitrary use of power. Bolívar spent his final days exiled from Bogotá and Caracas to Colombia's Caribbean coast. He died in 1830. His successor, general José Antonio Páez, finally consented to have his remains repatriated in 1842:

> He urged congress that it would be appropriate and a matter of political duty to restore Bolívar "so that in future public esteem for the memory of the Liberator may rest on the national vote legitimately expressed, and the demonstration of thanks and admiration for his great deeds of patriotism and humanity shall be in accord with the wishes of the legislators." At a time when civil unrest was never far away and the opposition readily reached for weapons rather than arguments, it was to the advantage of Páez and other politicians to bathe themselves in vicarious glory and associate themselves with the record of Bolívar.[29]

Páez activated a process from which Richard Nixon and George W. Bush may yet benefit, although it isn't likely to help Warren Harding at this late date. Political expediency won out over rivalries of the moment. Bolívar became Latin America's most common symbol of national liberation. Caracas centers its symbolic life on the Plaza Bolívar. By Centeno's count, "Every city except Montevideo and Asunción has a major statue to the Libertador, Simón Bolívar."[30] Since the 1840s, the name Bolívar has signified patriotism through most of Latin America.

That includes Venezuela, Bolívar's place of origin. During the early 1980s, a group of nationalist Venezuelan army officers organized a secret network called the Revolutionary Bolivarian Movement. Paratroop lieutenant colonel Hugo

Chávez became their leader. In 1992, the Bolivarians almost seized power in a military coup whose failure sent Chávez to prison. He was still in jail when another, more senior group of officers tried to seize power in November. They captured a TV station and broadcast a video. To the coup leader's consternation, a Chávez supporter substituted his own video, in which Chávez announced the government's fall. For that attempt, Chávez spent another two years in prison.

In 1993, while Chávez languished behind bars, the Venezuelan congress impeached President Carlos Andres Pérez for corruption, and removed him from office. But Pérez's successor, Rafael Caldera, soon faced a collapse of the country's banks, a surge of violent crime, rumors of new military coups, and charges of his own corruption. As Chávez left prison and entered politics, popular demands for political housecleaning swelled. Blame for the military plotter gave way to credit for the Bolivarian cleanser. By the 1998 presidential elections, the only serious opposition to former coup manager Chávez came from a former beauty queen. She dropped out of the running as the Chávez campaign gained widespread support.

Chávez billed himself as a populist, and won by a large majority. The following year, according to New York–based democracy monitoring organization Freedom House:

> Hugo Chávez, the coupist paratrooper-turned-politician who was elected president in a December 1998 landslide, spent most of 1999 dismantling Venezuela's political system of checks and balances, ostensibly to destroy a discredited two-party system that for four decades presided over several oil booms but has left four out of five Venezuelans impoverished. Early in the year, Congressional power was gutted, the judiciary was placed under

executive branch tutelage, and Chávez's army colleagues were given a far bigger say in the day-to-day running of the country. A constituent assembly dominated by Chávez followers drafted a new constitution that would make censorship of the press easier, allow a newly strengthened chief executive the right to dissolve Congress, and make it possible for Chávez to retain power until 2013. Congress and the Supreme Court were dismissed after Venezuelans approved the new constitution in a national referendum December 15.[31]

As Chávez came to power in 1999, street confrontations between his supporters and his opponents accelerated. The new president's state visit to Fidel Castro's officially socialist Cuba later the same year dramatized his plan to transform the government and its place in the world at large. He began squeezing the state oil company, Petróleos de Venezuela, for more of its revenues, and chipped away at its fabled autonomy. Chávez also revived an old, popular Venezuelan claim to a large chunk of western Guyana. Venezuela moved into a new stage of struggle over the country's future. Invocations of Bolívar became ever more frequent. Chávez claimed credit as a new liberator.

Over the next seven years, Chávez used his control over oil revenues to consolidate his power, to cramp his opposition, to sponsor populism elsewhere in Latin America, and even to hold off an increasingly hostile United States. He survived a U.S.-backed coup attempt in 2002, concerted resistance from the national oil company in 2002–2003, a general strike during the same period, and a U.S.-supported recall referendum in 2004. Step by step he responded with tightened repression. A Chávez-dominated legislature packed the Supreme Court, broadened prohibitions on insulting or showing disrespect for the president, and stepped up surveillance of mass media. Meanwhile, the courts prosecuted increasing numbers of regime opponents. All in the name of the Bolivarian Revolution.

Chávez enjoyed substantial support among Venezuela's numerous poor. He relied on his country's oil-generated wealth to stifle the opposition. His strategy won him a fat majority of 63 percent in his reelection campaign of 2006. The Bolivarian heritage still helped. Hugo Chávez's red shirts had become a visual symbol of his allegiance to Simón Bolívar, the liberator:

> In Caracas, voting at the Simón Bolívar elementary school in San Blas, a slum in the Petare district, proceeded calmly on Sunday morning. Once outside after voting, some voters put on red shirts and hats, indicating their support for Mr. Chávez. "I'm red, very red," said Carlos Gelvis, an unemployed man from Petare, in a reference to a refrain of Mr. Chávez's campaign.[32]

So long as Venezuelans could see parallels between the nineteenth-century Spanish empire and the twenty-first-century U.S. empire, they could accept the identification.

Credit and blame interacted once again. Chávez succeeded in identifying himself with Latin American liberation movements. He received credit for seizing national assets to enhance popular welfare. But he also succeeded in casting blame on that readily available enemy, the United States. His alliance with Fidel Castro's Cuba only reinforced the us-them boundary between socialist reformers and capitalist intruders. Here collective memory and current politics converged. They usually do.

RECONCILIATION, RETALIATION, OR REPARATION

As people are constructing collective memories of victory, loss, and blame, they sometimes settle for monuments and other reminders that comfort current politics on one side of the us-them line. Often, however, they activate one of three logics we have already seen in action: reconciliation, retaliation, or reparation.

Reconciliation typically involves some ritual encounter followed by a declaration that bygones should be bygones. Two friends blame each other for some bad outcome, then a third friend persuades them to make up. The victor treats the vanquished generously, and the two combatants go off for a ceremonial drink. In the most spectacular version, a truth and reconciliation commission brings together victims and perpetrators in a great civil conflict; perpetrators confess their crimes in response to some guarantees of immunity and absolution, before participants ritually symbolize forgiving and forgetting. If the reconciliation routine works, the parties then get on with collaboration in new collective enterprises.

Advocates of collective reconciliation often make three arguments for public apologies followed by mutual commitment: catharsis, justice, and expediency. Public discussion of past wrongs, goes the first line of reasoning, allows aggrieved people to stop grieving and wrongdoers to assuage their guilt. The justice argument fixes blame in the style of jail sentences, punitive damages, and shaming ceremonies when the perpetrator shows remorse and commitment to better behavior. The expediency principle focuses on the future: Unresolved conflicts impede cooperation. So let's agree on what happened and why, then get on with collective life.

Catharsis, justice, and expediency combined in 1997, when the German and Czech governments issued a joint declaration, "On Mutual Relations and Their Future Development." The governments were reaching agreement about two egregious wrongs: Nazi occupation of Czechoslovakia, and Czech expulsion of Sudeten Germans at the end of World War II.

> Both sides agree that injustice inflicted in the past belongs in the past, and will therefore orient their relations towards the future. Precisely because they remain conscious of the tragic chapters of their history, they are determined to continue to give priority to understanding and mutual agreement in the development of their relations, while each side remains committed to its legal system and respects the fact that the other side has a different legal position. Both sides therefore declare that they will not burden their relations with political and legal issues which stem from the past.[33]

Expediency outweighed catharsis and justice. The joint declaration made it easier for Germany to support admission of the Czech Republic to the European Union. Whether the declaration served catharsis and justice at all depends on the rough equation of Nazi occupation with German expulsion. Reconciliation often involves rough equations of wrong with wrong.

Collective *retaliation*, however, depends on a strict logic of tit for tat: you did us wrong, so you should suffer as badly. Where the line between perpetrators and victims is clear, collective retaliation has two advantages. First, it corresponds to an individual sense of justice that cuts across cultures and historical periods. Second, it involves a simple calculus: you stole our cow, we take your cow. But it also has two enormous disadvantages. It allows the rasher members of one side to score hero points by acting aggressively against vulnerable members of the other side. And it escalates easily, because members of a newly victimized side so regularly interpret a retaliatory attack as disproportionate to the offense and as a threat to their side's credibility and honor.

We know about escalation from legendary feuds between the Montagues and Capulets or the Hatfields and McCoys. Blood feuds once disfigured large areas of Southern Europe.[34] In the Balkan blood feud, a forbidden cross-boundary inter-action initiated retaliation by members of the wronged party. The wronged group sought visible satisfaction for the wrong by inflicting some specified kind of harm on the boundary's other side.

The boundary separated lineages, and the acting groups were usually younger males of each lineage. Feud-triggering interactions included:

- calling a man a liar in the presence of other men

- killing a man

- killing a house's guard dog within the house's territory

- insulting a man's wife

- taking his weapons

- violating his hospitality, for example by stealing from a host[35]

Any of these interactions impugned the honor not only of the man, but also of his lineage. It put lineage members "in blood" with a neighboring lineage. Lineage members took on the obligation to hunt down and kill an adult male member of the offending lineage. At that point the killer(s) announced the feat, then could request a truce between the lineages for some period. At the truce's expiration, a new round could begin as members of the lineage that started the interaction set out to avenge their loss.

Powerful third parties sometimes intervened to contain or suppress a feud when killing escalated. But without a firm stopping rule comparable to the clock's running out in football, and in the absence of strong governments, ritual killing could continue for years.

Blood feuds once existed widely in other parts of Europe. Remember that German generals Armin and Segestes were feuding in 9 A.D. over Armin's capture of Segestes's daughter. But starting in the sixteenth and seventeenth centuries western European governments either suppressed feuds or channeled them into judicial proceedings from which rulers could collect significant fines or confiscations of property.[36] In the Balkans, central governments rarely achieved that kind of control. Blood feuds continued to occur there until the recent past. Collective retaliation often causes long-lasting damage.

Reparations follow a modified logic of tit for tat: you did us wrong, so you should compensate us proportionately. Along the way, you should apologize for doing us wrong. Discussing books on reparations, *Times Literary Supplement* critic David Lowenthal deplored the practice. Forgetting that U.S. president Ronald Reagan had apologized in 1988 to Japanese Americans the government had incarcerated during World War II, Lowenthal complained that

> The Age of Apology came to a head with 1990s contrition chic: Bill Clinton apologized for slavery, Tony Blair for the Irish Famine, the Pope for the Crusades, Australia declared a "National Sorry Day" for past mistreatment of

Aborigines, with little to show by way of present improvement. Posthumous mea culpas dispense cheap cheer. They show how venial are our own sins by comparison with our forebears' crimes. Past sinners are excoriated for not thinking and acting as right-minded people do today. Censorious tracts name and shame perpetrators of history's atrocities, demanding remorse and redress for victims' heirs.[37]

The complications start there. Who are the victims? Who are the perpetrators? Do today's descendants or relatives of victims deserve compensation for the victims' losses? Do today's descendants or relatives of perpetrators bear responsibility for the perpetrators' evils? What counts as adequate compensation? Compensation for 9/11 losses begins to look simple when compared to reparations for losses that extend over generations.

Yet in recent years demands for collective reparations have become common and reputable in the United States and elsewhere. Sociologist John Torpey asks why. He underlines confluence of two main factors: compensation of Jews and the state of Israel for the Holocaust and generalization of the practice to compensation paid by states to groups that have suffered wrongs in both war and peace. "The spread of reparations," Torpey concludes,

> thus parallels the rise of human rights thinking, the emergence of substate groups and individuals as subjects of international law, and the juridification of politics in general.[38]

Once one group successfully presses a claim for recognition of its victimization, other groups can follow the same path. Demands for reparations typically combine the principles of catharsis, justice, and expediency. Substantial payments, in this view, allow victims to move past victimization and perpetrators to purge their guilt. Categories of people who have suffered call for just compensation that requires today's members of oppressing groups to feel some measure of the pain they or their predecessors have inflicted. Political organizers say that reparations will promote reconciliation and future collaboration.

No doubt these outcomes do sometimes occur. But reparations politics involves two great dangers. First, it provides incentives for people including lawyers and advocates to hoard rewards for themselves rather than redistributing them to genuine victims. Second, it reinforces us-them boundaries instead of dissolving them. When, for example, Native Americans receive compensation for past wrongs in the form of property rights, exemption from taxes, and direct governmental subsidies, both effects often happen. Lobbyists and lawyers make money as differences between Native Americans and other Americans sharpen.[39]

The public assignment of credit and blame has profound implications for democracy. Democracy can live with us-them differences. It provides a means of temporarily bridging social differences by class, gender, religion, or race without abolishing them. But writing us-them divisions into law and politics undermines democracy.[40] That is why we count the abolitions of property requirements, of racial exclusions, and of male-only electorates as historical triumphs for democracy.

Credit and blame pose difficult problems for democracy. As we have seen throughout this book, all of us spend much of our lives assigning credit and blame. Justice matters to everyday personal relations as it matters to public life. Those of us who seek the proper assignment of credit and blame often turn to the courts, to legislatures, and to other governmental institutions to back up our judgments of right and wrong. Americans and their lawyers regularly call for courts to award not only material compensation but punitive damages.[41] Within limits, successful pursuit of legal redress reinforces democracy. It establishes that even relatively powerless people can get justice and that government officials care about their welfare.

Beyond those limits, however, use of public power to fix credit and blame writes us-them divisions into political life. It also reinforces the operation of the same divisions in private life. After all, the vengeance called for by the Hermann Monument helped bring on World War I and the Nazi rise to power after the German loss of World War I. The struggle over Sacré Coeur and the Catholic Church's place in French public life promoted the virulent anti-Semitism of the Dreyfus case twenty years later, helped produce a great crisis of state-church relations in 1905–1906, and left echoes in France's conservative revival during the 1930s and 1940s. Be very careful when you call for the authorities to back up your assignments of credit and blame.

NOTES

1. CREDIT, BLAME, AND SOCIAL LIFE

1. Dostoevsky 1964: 1–2.
2. Dostoevsky 1964: 521.
3. Boltanski and Thévenot 2006.
4. Wilson 2006: 818.
5. Wilson 2006: 829–830.
6. Cushman 2006, Hauser 2006.
7. Brennan and Pettit 2004.
8. ICJT 2007.
9. USIP 2005: 2.
10. Rotberg 2006: 37–38.
11. Ramsey and Abrams 2001: 385–388.
12. Lawcopedia 2006, Tilly 2006a, chapter 4.
13. Trump 2004: 3.
14. Welch 2005: 34–35.
15. Thomas 2006: C5.
16. Ashforth 2000: 21–22.
17. Ashforth 2005: xiii–xiv.
18. Tilly 2002a, 2006a.
19. Tilly 1995b, 1996.
20. Maier 1997: 240–241.
21. Maier 1997: 105–142.
22. Washington 1796: 2.
23. Washington 1796: 4.
24. White House 2002: 3.
25. White House 2002: 5, 9.

26. Fukuyama 2006: 83.

27. See, e.g., Koch 2004, Wegner 2002.

2. JUSTICE

1. Buell-Wilson 2006: 5–6.

2. Buell-Wilson 2006: 1.

3. AP 2004: 2.

4. Copley 2004: 2.

5. Feigenson 2000: 5.

6. Buell-Wilson 2006: 7.

7. Moran 2006: 2.

8. Feigenson 2000: 89.

9. Abbott 2002: 3.

10. Abbott 2002: 13.

11. Abbott 2002: 16.

12. Iyengar 1991.

13. Mazie 2005: 1.

14. Verni 2006.

15. Mansnerus 2006.

16. Justice 2004.

17. Feigenson 2000: 148.

18. Feigenson 2000: 149.

19. Feigenson 2000: 104–108.

20. Friedman 1985: 43.

21. Tilly 2003a, chapter 8.

22. Scott 1985.

23. Brown 1975, Grimsted 1998, McKivigan and Harrold 1999.

24. Narayan and Petesch 2002: 71.

25. Ashforth 2005: 102, Bozzoli 2004.

26. Tilly 2007.

27. Pettai 2003, Raun 1997.

28. Goodin et al. 1999, Lindert 2004.

29. Henrich et al. 2004: 8.

30. Henrich et al. 2004: 11–13; see also Henrich et al. 2006, Samuelson 2005.

31. see Tilly 2001.
32. Henrich et al. 2004: 28–38.
33. Bowles 2006.
34. Nasrallah 2006.
35. ABC 2006: 3.
36. Grimson 1999: 38.
37. Baily 1999, Sabato 2001.
38. Grimson 1999: 71–72.
39. English 2005: 190–191.
40. Collins 1998.
41. Zuckerman 1996: 231.

3. CREDIT

1. Kinn and Piazza 2002: 12.
2. English 2005: 84.
3. English 2005: 161.
4. Hoffman 2006.
5. Levy 2003: 330.
6. Levy 2003: 16.
7. Oscarworld 2006.
8. Kandel 2006: 393–394.
9. Frank and Cook 1995.
10. Nasar and Gruber 2006: 15.
11. Stroock 2006.
12. National Honor Society 2006.
13. Pellisson-Fontainer and d'Olivet 1858: I, 16–17.
14. Hahn 1971: chapter 3.
15. Roche 1978: I, 19–20.
16. Roche 1978: I, 391.
17. Tilly 1986: 153–156.
18. Bruce 1993: 204.
19. Education 1999: 1–2.
20. Nooyi 2005: 2–3.
21. Nooyi 2005: 4.

22. Tilly 1998, chapter 3. See, for example, the fierce dispute that arose in 2006 over UCLA law professor Richard Sander's claim that major law firms were hiring black lawyers who had significantly lower grade averages than their non-black counterparts, and that the black lawyers' inferior qualifications were causing partners to assign them disproportionately to "grunt work," which in turn shifted black lawyers from partnership tracks and caused them to drop out disproportionately before becoming eligible for partnerships. Critics didn't dispute the lower grades or the average differences in job assignments, but they challenged the causal account energetically: Sander 2006, Liptak 2006, Coleman and Gulati 2006.

23. Carré, Holgate, and Tilly 2005.

24. District Court 2003: 52.

25. Drogin 2003: 12–18.

26. Besen and Kimmel 2006: 178.

27. Roth 2006: 10.

28. Gilfoyle 2006: 318–319.

4. BLAME

1. Belluck 2006.

2. Belluck 2006.

3. Weissenstein 2003.

4. Belluck 2006.

5. CBS 2003.

6. Rosenbaum 2004: 23.

7. Zelizer 1985: 32.

8. Zelizer 1985: 142–143.

9. Verni 2006.

10. Zelizer 1985: 159.

11. Peyser 2006: 2.

12. Nursing Advocacy 2006.

13. Italiano 2006: 1.

14. Italiano 2006: 2.

15. Heimer and Staffen 1998: 107.

16. Heimer and Staffen 1998: 106.

17. Masters 2005: 120.

18. Masters 2005: 122.

19. Masters 2005: 122.

20. For general discussions of us-them boundaries, see Tilly 2005b.

21. Gilbert 1941: 330–332.

22. Axelrod 1984: viii.

23. Hagan 1994: 164.

24. Hagan 1994: 163.

25. Human Rights Watch 2002, Schneider 1998, Sentencing Commission 1995.

26. Commission 2004: 285–315.

27. See, for example, www.911truth.org. For skeptical summaries of major conspiracy theories, see Kean and Hamilton 2006: 252–256, Cockburn 2006.

28. Zelizer 2005: 275–278.

29. Breitweiser 2006: 67.

30. Breitweiser 2006: 76–77, 81–82.

31. Breitweiser 2006: 80–81.

32. Breitweiser 2006: 110–117.

33. Kean and Hamilton 2006: 16.

34. Breitweiser 2006: 137–140.

35. Kean and Hamilton 2006: 5–6, 12.

36. Kleinberg 2003: 2.

37. Kean and Hamilton 2006: 229.

38. Kean and Hamilton 2006: 31, 199–200.

39. Commission 2004. In November 2006, after a public flap over his pressing for action on the Arab-Israeli conflict, Zelikow resigned from his State Department post and returned to his endowed history chair at the University of Virginia.

40. For what they are worth, you can find analyses of terrorism in Tilly 2002b, 2004b, 2005a, and 2006b: 137–150.

41. DeMott 2004: 2.

42. Kean and Hamilton 206: 276.

5. MEMORIES OF VICTORY, LOSS, AND BLAME

1. Tacitus 2006: 37.

2. An Arminius. Über den Rhein hast du einst Roms Legionen getrieben, und Germanien dankt dir, dass es heute noch ist. Schwinge ferner dein Schwert, wenn Frankreichs plündernde Horden gierig lechzend des Rheins heimische Gauen bedrohn.

3. Harvey 1985: 226.

4. Harvey 1985: 239.

5. Emery 2001: 67.

6. Emery 2001: 70.

7. Kandel 2006.

8. Tilly 1994, 2003b.

9. Mayo 1988: 72.

10. Barber 1949.

11. Mayo 1988: 204.

12. Homer News 2003.

13. McKinley 2006.

14. McKinley 2006.

15. Wall Street Journal 2000. The poll omitted William Henry Harrison and James Garfield because of their very short presidential terms.

16. Fine 2001: 79.

17. Fine 2001: 64.

18. Schwartz 2000, chapter 2.

19. Hendren 2006.

20. Quinnipiac 2006: 1.

21. Quinnipiac 2006: 9.

22. Quinnipiac 2006: 9.

23. Micklethwait 2006: 11

24. New York Times 1971: xi.

25. Schlesinger 1965. Revised versions of the book remain in print after 40 years.

26. Centeno 2002: 198.

27. Centeno 2002: 204.

28. Centeno 2002: 204.

29. Lynch 2006: 300.
30. Centeno 2002: 213.
31. Karatnycky 2000: 522.
32. Romero 2006.
33. Barkan and Karn 2006: 9.
34. Allcock 2000: 388–390; see also Blok 2001, Boehm 1987, Malcolm 1996, 1998, Mazower 2000.
35. Malcolm 1998: 18–21.
36. Ylikangas, Karonen and Lehti 2001.
37. Lowenthal 2006: 3.
38. Torpey 2006: 159.
39. Torpey 2006: 60–62.
40. Tilly 2007, chapter 5.
41. Greenhouse 2006; see, e.g., SourceWatch 2006.

REFERENCES

Abbott, H. Porter (2002): *The Cambridge Introduction to Narrative*. Cambridge: Cambridge University Press.

ABC (2006): "Israel-Lebanon Cease-Fire Goes into Effect," ABC News International, abcnews.go.com/International/Mideast/wireStory?id= 2309811, viewed 24 August 2006.

Allcock, John B. (2000): *Explaining Yugoslavia*. New York: Columbia University Press.

AP (2004): "Judge Reduces Damage Award for Victim of Ford Explorer Crash," Associated Press, 19 August, from LexisNexis 17 August 2006.

Ashforth, Adam (2000): *Madumo: A Man Bewitched*. Chicago: University of Chicago Press.

—— (2005): *Witchcraft, Violence, and Democracy in South Africa*. Chicago: University of Chicago Press.

Axelrod, Robert (1984): *The Evolution of Cooperation*. New York: Basic Books.

Baily, Samuel L. (1999): *Immigrants in the Land of Promise: Italians in Buenos Aires and New York City, 1870–1914*. Ithaca, NY: Cornell University Press.

Barber, Bernard (1949): "Place, Symbol, and Utilitarian Function in War Memorials," *Social Forces* 28: 64–68.

Barkan, Elazar, and Alexander Karn (2006): "Group Apology as an Ethical Imperative," in Elazar Barkan and Alexander Karn, eds., *Taking Wrongs Seriously: Apologies and Reconciliation*. Stanford, CA: Stanford University Press.

Belluck, Pam (2006): "Sentencing in Deadly Nightclub Fire Only Adds to Anguish of Victims and Kin," *New York Times* online, 30 September 2006.

Besen, Yasemin, and Michael S. Kimmel (2006): "At Sam's Club, No Girls Allowed: The Lived Experience of Sex Discrimination," *Equal Opportunities International* 25: 172–187.

Blok, Anton (2001): *Honour and Violence.* Cambridge: Polity.

Boehm, Christopher (1987): *Blood Revenge: The Enactment and Management of Conflict in Montenegro and Other Tribal Societies.* Philadelphia: University of Pennsylvania Press. First published by University Press of Kansas, 1984.

Boltanski, Luc, and Laurent Thévenot (2006): *On Justification: Economies of Worth.* Princeton, NJ: Princeton University Press.

Bowles, Samuel (2006): "Group Competition, Reproductive Leveling, and the Evolution of Human Altruism," *Science* 314: 1569–1572.

Bozzoli, Belinda (2004): *Theatres of Struggle and the End of Apartheid.* Edinburgh: Edinburgh University Press for the International African Institute, London.

Breitweiser, Kristen (2006): *Wake-Up Call: The Political Education of a 9/11 Widow.* New York: Warner Books.

Brennan, Geoffrey, and Philip Pettit (2004): *The Economy of Esteem: An Essay on Civil and Political Society.* Oxford: Oxford University Press.

Brown, Richard Maxwell (1975): *Strain of Violence: Historical Studies of American Violence and Vigilantism.* New York: Oxford University Press.

Bruce, Robert V. (1993): "The Misfire of Civil War R&D," in John A. Lynn, ed., *Feeding Mars: Logistics in Western Warfare from the Middle Ages to the Present.* Boulder, CO: Westview.

Buell-Wilson (2006): 2006 Cal. App. Lexis 1089; 2006 Daily Journal DAR 9367, Benetta Buell-Wilson et al., v. Ford Motor Company et al., from LexisNexis 17 August 2006.

Carré, Françoise, Brandynn Holgate, and Chris Tilly (2005): "What's Happening to Retail Jobs? Wages, Gender, and Corporate

Strategy," presented to the annual meetings of the International Association for Feminist Economics and the Labor and Employment Relations Association, Boston, January 2005.

CBS (2003): "Panel Hears of Club Fire Horror," *CBS News* online, 27 February 2003.

Centeno, Miguel (2002): *Blood and Debt: War and the Nation-State in Latin America.* University Park: Pennsylvania State University Press.

Cockburn, Alexander (2006): "Scepticisme ou occultisme? Le complot du 11-Septembre n'aura pas lieu," *Le Monde diplomatique* December 2006: 3.

Coleman, James E. Jr., and Mitu Gulati (2006): "A Response to Professor Sander: Is it Really All about the Grades?" *North Carolina Law Review* 84: 1823–1839.

Collins, Randall (1998): *The Sociology of Philosophies: A Global Theory of Intellectual Change.* Cambridge, MA: Harvard University Press.

Commission (2004) (National Commission on Terrorist Attacks Upon the United States): *The 9/11 Commission Report.* New York: Norton.

Copley (2004): "Award Reduced in Explorer Rollover," Copley News Service 20 August, from LexisNexis 17 August 2006.

Cushman, Fiery (2006): "The Declaration of Independence—A Lab Report," *In Character* 3, no. 1 (Fall): 50–61.

DeMott, Benjamin (2004): "Whitewash as Public Service: How the 9/11 Commission Report Defrauds the Nation," *Harper's* online edition, www.harpers.org/WhitewashAsPublicService.html, viewed 5 November 2005.

District Court (2003): United States District Court, Northern District of California, before the Honorable Martin J. Jenkins, Judge, transcript of proceedings, 24 September 2003, www.walmartclass.com/walmartclass94.pl, viewed 24 September 2006.

Dostoevsky, Feodor (1964): *Crime and Punishment.* New York: W.W. Norton. First published 1866–1867.

Drogin, Richard (2003): "Statistical Analysis of Gender Patterns in Wal-Mart Workforce," www.walmartclass.com/staticdata/reports, viewed 24 September 2006.

Education (1999) (U.S. Department of Education): "Taking Responsibility for Ending Social Promotion, Executive Summary," www.ed.gov/pubs/socialpromotion/execsum.html, viewed 21 September 2006.

Emery, Elizabeth (2001): "The Power of the Pen: Emile Zola Takes on the Sacré-Coeur Basilica," in Buford Norman, ed., *The Documentary Impulse in French Literature.* Amsterdam and Atlanta, GA: Editions Rodopi.

English, James F. (2005): *The Economy of Prestige: Prizes, Awards, and the Circulation of Cultural Value.* Cambridge, MA: Harvard University Press.

Feigenson, Neal (2000): *Legal Blame: How Jurors Think and Talk About Accidents.* Washington, DC: American Psychological Association.

Fine, Gary Alan (2001): *Difficult Reputations: Collective Memories of the Evil, Inept, and Controversial.* Chicago: University of Chicago Press.

Frank, Robert H., and Philip J. Cook (1995): *The Winner-Take-All Society: How More and More Americans Compete for Ever Fewer and Bigger Prizes, Encouraging Economic Waste, Income Inequality, and an Impoverished Cultural Life.* New York: Free Press.

Friedman, Lawrence M. (1985): *Total Justice.* New York: Russell Sage Foundation.

Fukuyama, Francis (2006): *America at the Crossroads: Democracy, Power, and the Neoconservative Legacy.* New Haven, CT: Yale University Press.

Gilbert, W.S. (1941): *The Complete Plays of Gilbert and Sullivan.* New York: W.W. Norton.

Gilfoyle, Timothy J. (2006): *A Pickpocket's Tale: The Underworld of Nineteenth-Century New York.* New York: Norton.

Goodin, Robert E., Bruce Headey, Ruud Muffels, and Henk-Jan Dirven (1999): *The Real Worlds of Welfare Capitalism.* Cambridge: Cambridge University Press.

Greenhouse, Linda (2006): "Justices Weigh Limits on Punitive Damages," *New York Times* online edition, 1 November, viewed 1 November 2006.

Grimson, Alejandro (1999): *Relatos de la diferencia y la igualdad: Los bolivianos en Buenos Aires.* Buenos Aires: Editorial Universitaria de Buenos Aires.

Grimsted, David (1998): *American Mobbing, 1828–1861: Toward Civil War.* New York: Oxford University Press.

Hagan, John (1994): *Crime and Disrepute.* Thousand Oaks, CA: Pine Forge Press.

Hahn, Roger (1971): *The Anatomy of a Scientific Institution: The Paris Academy of Sciences, 1666–1803.* Berkeley: University of California Press.

Harvey, David (1985): *Consciousness and the Urban Experience: Studies in the History and Theory of Capitalist Urbanization.* Baltimore: Johns Hopkins University Press.

Hauser, Marc D. (2006): *Moral Minds: How Nature Designed Our Universal Sense of Right and Wrong.* New York: HarperCollins.

Heimer, Carol A., and Lisa R. Staffen (1998): *For the Sake of the Children: The Social Organization of Responsibility in the Hospital and the Home.* Chicago: University of Chicago Press.

Hendren, John (2006): "War Casts Heavy Shadow on Lame-Duck President," ABC News online, www.abcnews.go.com/Politics/story?id=2732453&page=1, viewed 1 January 2007.

Henrich, Joseph, Robert Boyd, Samuel Bowles, Colin Camerer, Ernst Fehr, and Herbert Gintis, eds. (2004): *Foundations of Human Sociality: Economic Experiments and Ethnographic Evidence from Fifteen Small-Scale Societies.* Oxford: Oxford University Press.

Henrich, Joseph, et al. (2006): "Costly Punishment across Human Societies," *Science* 312: 1767–1770.

Hoffman, Philip Seymour (2006): "Winner, Actor in a Leading Role," www.oscars.org/78academyawards/winners/01_lead_actor .html, viewed 6 September 2006.

Homer News (2003): "War Prompts Street Demonstrations," HomerNews.com, 3 April.

Human Rights Watch (2002): "Race and Incarceration in the United States: Human Rights Watch Press Backgrounder," www .hrw.org/backgrounder/usa/race, viewed 8 November 2006.

ICTJ (2007): International Center for Transitional Justice, "Mission and History," www.ictj.org/en/about/mission/, viewed 16 February 2007.

Italiano, Laura (2006): "Mom Hurls Wrath at Brutal Nanny," *New York Post* online edition, 27 October 2006, viewed 6 November 2006.

Iyengar, Shanto (1991): *Is Anyone Responsible? How Television Frames Political Issues.* Chicago: University of Chicago Press.

Jasso, Guillermina (1999): "How Much Injustice Is There in the World? Two New Justice Indexes," *American Sociological Review* 64: 133–168.

Justice (2004) (U.S. Department of Justice, Bureau of Justice Statistics): "Tort Trials and Verdicts in Large Counties, 2001," November 2004, www.ojp.usdoj.gov/bjs/pub/ascii/ttvic01.txt, viewed 18 August 2006.

Kandel, Eric R. (2006): *In Search of Memory: The Emergence of a New Science of Mind.* New York: W.W. Norton.

Karatnycky, Adrian, ed. (2000): *Freedom in the World: The Annual Survey of Political Rights and Civil Liberties 1999–2000.* New York: Freedom House.

Kean, Thomas H., and Lee H. Hamilton (2006) (with Benjamin Rhodes): *Without Precedent: The Inside Story of the 9/11 Commission.* New York: Alfred A. Knopf.

Kinn, Gail, and Jim Piazza (2002): *The Academy Awards: The Complete History of Oscar.* New York: Black Dog and Leventhal.

Kleinberg, Mindy (2003): "Statement of Mindy Kleinberg to the National Commission on Terrorist Attacks upon the United

States, March 31, 2003," www.9-11commission.gov/hearings/ hearing1/witness_kleinberg.html, viewed 10 November 2003.

Koch, Christof (2004): *The Quest for Consciousness: A Neurobiological Approach.* Englewood, CO: Roberts and Company.

Lawcopedia (2006): The 'Lectric Law Library *Lawcopedia's* Law & Medicine Medical Malpractice Topic Area, www.lectlaw.com/ tmed.html, viewed 10 August 2006.

Levy, Emanuel (2003): *All about Oscar: The History and Politics of the Academy Awards.* New York: Continuum.

Lindert, Peter H. (2004): *Growing Public: Social Spending and Economic Growth since the Eighteenth Century.* 2 vols. Cambridge: Cambridge University Press.

Liptak, Adam (2006): "Lawyers Debate Why Blacks Lag at Major Firms," *New York Times* online edition, 29 November.

Lowenthal, David (2006): "Beyond Repair," *Times Literary Supplement,* 24 November, 3–4.

Lynch, John (2006): *Simón Bolívar: A Life.* New Haven, CT: Yale University Press.

Maier, Pauline (1997): *American Scripture: Making the Declaration of Independence.* New York: Alfred A. Knopf.

Malcolm, Noel (1996): *Bosnia: A Short History.* Revised edition. New York: New York University Press. First published in 1994.

—— (1998): *Kosovo: A Short History.* New York: New York University Press.

Mansnerus, Laura (2006): "Court Overturns Jury Award against Stadium Concessionaire," *New York Times,* 4 August, B3.

Masters, Alexander (2005): *Stuart: A Life Backwards.* New York: Delacorte Press.

Mayo, James M. (1988): *War Memorials as Political Landscape: The American Experience and Beyond.* New York: Praeger.

Mazie (2005): "$135 Million Jury Verdict for Alcohol Liability," www.injurylawyernewjersey.com/article19.html, viewed 18 August 2006.

Mazower, Mark (2000): *The Balkans: A Short History.* New York: Modern Library.

McKinley, Jesse (2006): "Homemade Memorial Stirs Opposing Passions on Iraq," *New York Times*, 3 December, N30.

McKivigan, John R., and Stanley Harrold, eds. (1999): *Antislavery Violence: Sectional, Racial, and Cultural Conflict in Antebellum America*. Knoxville: University of Tennessee Press.

Mellies, Dirk (2001): "Die Bau- und Forschungsgeschichte des Hermannsdenkmales—ein Resümée," in Stefanie Lux-Althoff, ed., *125 Jahre Hermannsdenkmal: Nationaldenkmale im historischen und politischen Kontext*. Lemgo: Institut für Lippische Landeskunde.

Micklethwait, John (2006): "It's Still Down to George Bush," *The World in 2007*. London: The Economist.

Moran, Greg (2006): "Jury's Award in Rollover Cut in Half: But Ford's Request for a New Trial Fails," *San Diego Union-Tribune*, 20 July, B-1, from LexisNexis 17 August 2006.

Narayan, Deepa, and Patti Petesch, eds. (2002): *Voices of the Poor: From Many Lands*. Washington, DC: World Bank and New York: Oxford University Press.

Nasar, Sylvia, and David Gruber (2006): "Manifold Destiny: A Legendary Problem and the Battle over Who Solved It," New Yorker Printables 28 August, www.newyorker.com/printables/fact/060828fa_fact2, viewed 7 September 2006.

Nasrallah (2006): "Hizbollah Declares Victory," Yahoo! News 14 August, news.yahoo.com/s/nm/20060814/ts_nm/mideast_nasrallah_de_4, viewed 24 August 2006.

National Honor Society (2006): "Membership," www.nhs.us, viewed 18 September 2006.

New York Times (1971): *The Pentagon Papers*. Toronto, New York, and London: Bantam Books.

Nooyi, Indra (2005): "Indra Nooyi's Graduation Remarks," *Business Week Online*, 20 May, www.businessweek.com/bwdaily/dnflash/may2005/nf200505, viewed 23 September 2006.

Nursing Advocacy (2006): Center for Nursing Advocacy, "Nursing the Baby Nurses," www.nursingadvocacy.org/cgi-bin/, viewed 8 November 2006.

Oscarworld (2006): "Memorable Oscar Speeches," www.oscarworld .net/oscarspeeches.asp, viewed 7 September 2006.

Pellisson-Fontainer and Pierre Joseph d'Olivet (1858): *Histoire de l'Académie française*. Paris: Didier. 2 vols. Nineteenth-century edition of two books originally published in 1658 and 1729.

Pettai, Vello (2003): "Framing the Past as Future: The Power of Legal Restorationism in Estonia," unpublished doctoral dissertation in political science, Columbia University.

Peyser, Andrea (2006): "'I'll Blame Self Until I Die,'" *New York Post* online edition, 30 October, www.nypost.com, viewed 6 November 2006.

Quinnipiac (2006): "Bush Tops List As U.S. Voters Name Worst President, Quinnipiac University National Poll Finds; Reagan, Clinton Top List as Best in 61 Years," www.quinnipiac.edu/ x1284.xml, viewed 3 December 2006.

Ramsey, Sarah H., and Douglas E. Abrams (2001): *Children and the Law in a Nutshell.* St. Paul, MN: West Group.

Raun, Toivo U. (1997): "Democratization and Political Development in Estonia, 1987–96," in Karen Dawisha and Bruce Parrott, eds., *The Consolidation of Democracy in East-Central Europe.* Cambridge: Cambridge University Press.

Roche, Daniel (1978): *Le siècle des Lumières en province: Académies et academicians provinciaux, 1680–1789.* 2 vols. Paris: Mouton.

Romero, Simon (2006): "Chávez Wins Easily in Venezuela, but Opposition Protests," *New York Times*, 4 December, A10.

Rosenbaum, Thane (2004): *The Myth of Moral Justice: Why Our Legal System Fails to Do What's Right.* New York: HarperCollins.

Rotberg, Robert (2006): "Apology, Truth Commissions, and Intrastate Conflict," in Elazar Barkan and Alexander Karn, eds., *Taking Wrongs Seriously: Apologies and Reconciliation.* Stanford, CA: Stanford University Press.

Roth, Philip (2006): *Everyman.* Boston: Houghton Mifflin.

Sabato, Hilda (2001): *The Many and the Few: Political Participation in Republican Buenos Aires.* Stanford, CA: Stanford University Press.

Samuelson, Larry (2005): "Foundations of Human Sociality: A Review Essay," *Journal of Economic Literature* 43: 488–497.

Sander, Richard H. (2006): "The Racial Paradox of the Corporate Law Firm," *North Carolina Law Review* 84: 1755–1822.

Schlesinger, Arthur M., Jr. (1965): *A Thousand Days: John F. Kennedy in the White House*. Boston: Houghton Mifflin.

Schneider, Cathy (1998): "Racism, Drug Policy and AIDS," *Political Science Quarterly* 113: 427–446.

Schwartz, Barry (2000): *Abraham Lincoln and the Forge of National Memory*. Chicago: University of Chicago Press.

Scott, James (1985): *Weapons of the Weak: Everyday Forms of Peasant Resistance*. New Haven, CT: Yale University Press.

Sentencing Commission (1995): *Special Report to the Congress: Cocaine and Federal Sentencing Policy*. Washington, DC: United States Sentencing Commission.

Sourcewatch (2006): "Monsanto and the Pollution of Anniston, Alabama," www.sourcewatch.org/index.php, viewed 19 July 2006.

Stroock, Daniel (2006): "A Matter of Math," *New Yorker*, 11 September, 7.

Tacitus (2006): *Complete Works of Tacitus*. New York: The Modern Library.

Thomas, Landon, Jr. (2006): "On the Road with Jack and Suzy: Things to Do, Places to Go, Money to Make," *New York Times*, 2 November, C1, C5.

Tilly, Charles (1986): *The Contentious French*. Cambridge, MA: Harvard University Press.

—— (1994): "Afterword: Political Memories in Space and Time," in Jonathan Boyarin, ed., *Remapping Memory: The Politics of TimeSpace*. Minneapolis: University of Minnesota Press.

—— (1995a): *Popular Contention in Great Britain, 1758–1834*. Cambridge, MA: Harvard University Press.

—— (1995b): "To Explain Political Processes," *American Journal of Sociology* 100: 1594–1610.

—— (1996): "Invisible Elbow," *Sociological Forum* 11: 589–601.

—— (1997): "Parliamentarization of Popular Contention in Great Britain, 1758–1834," *Theory and Society* 26: 245–273.

—— (1998): *Durable Inequality*. Berkeley: University of California Press.

—— (2001): "Do unto Others," in Marco Giugni and Florence Passy, eds., *Political Altruism? The Solidarity Movement in International Perspective*. Lanham, MD: Rowman & Littlefield.

—— (2002a): *Stories, Identities, and Political Change*. Lanham, MD: Rowman & Littlefield.

—— (2002b): "Violence, Terror, and Politics as Usual," *Boston Review* 27, nos. 3–4: 21–24.

—— (2003a): *The Politics of Collective Violence*. Cambridge: Cambridge University Press.

—— (2003b): "Afterword: Borges and Brass," in Jeffrey K. Olick, ed, *States of Memory: Continuities, Conflicts, and Transformations in National Retrospection*. Durham, NC: Duke University Press.

—— (2004a): "Social Boundary Mechanisms," *Philosophy of the Social Sciences* 34: 211–236.

—— (2004b): "Terror, Terrorism, Terrorists," *Sociological Theory* 22: 5–13.

—— (2005a): "Terror as Strategy and Relational Process," *International Journal of Comparative Sociology* 46: 11–32.

—— (2005b): *Identities, Boundaries, and Social Ties*. Boulder, CO: Paradigm Publishers.

—— (2006a): *Why?* Princeton: Princeton University Press.

—— (2006b): *Regimes and Repertoires*. Chicago: University of Chicago Press.

—— (2007): *Democracy*. Cambridge: Cambridge University Press.

Torpey, John (2006): *Making Whole What Has Been Smashed: On Reparations Politics*. Cambridge, MA: Harvard University Press.

Trump, Donald J. (2004) (with Meredith McIver): *How to Get Rich*. New York: Random House.

USIP (2005) (United States Institute of Peace): "Truth Commissions Digital Collection," www.usip.org/library/truth.html, viewed 8 August 2006.

Verni (2006): 2006 N.J. Super. Lexis 229, Antonia Verni et al. v. Harry M. Stevens Inc. et al., from LexisNexis 18 August 2006.

Wall Street Journal (2000): "Hail to the Chief," www.opinionjournal.com/hail/, viewed 3 December 2006.

Washington (1796): "George Washington's Farewell Address," www.earlyamerica.com/earlyamerica/milestones/farewell/text.html, viewed 16 August 2006.

Wegner, Daniel M. (2002): *The Illusion of Conscious Will*. Cambridge, MA: MIT Press.

Weissenstein, Michael (2003): "Fire Inspections Questioned," *Woonsocket Call* online, March 4, 2003.

Welch, Jack (2005) (with Suzy Welch): *Winning*. New York: HarperBusiness.

White House (2002): The National Security Strategy of the United States of America, www.whitehouse.gov/nsc/nssall.html, viewed 17 August 2006.

Wilson, Edward O., ed. (2006): *From So Simple a Beginning: The Four Great Books of Charles Darwin*. New York: W.W. Norton.

Ylikangas, Heikki, Petri Karonen, and Martti Lehti (2001): *Five Centuries of Violence in Finland and the Baltic Area*. Columbus: Ohio State University Press.

Zelizer, Viviana A. (1985): *Pricing the Priceless Child: The Changing Social Value of Children*. New York: Basic Books.

—— (2005): *The Purchase of Intimacy*. Princeton, NJ: Princeton University Press.

Zuckerman, Harriet (1996): *Scientific Elite: Nobel Laureates in the United States*. Revised edition. New Brunswick, NJ: Transaction. First published in 1977.

INDEX

Abbott, Porter, 39–40

Académie Française (French Academy), 72–75

Academy Awards, 61–66

Academy of Motion Picture Arts and Sciences, 61, 66

Adams, John, 23–24

agency: in the Buell-Wilson case, 37–38; as component of justice detector, 35–36; as element of judging credit and blame, 11–16, 34, 103; in stories assigning blame/credit, 38–42

Agnew, Spiro, 136

Alacoque, Marguerite-Marie, 123

Allick, Noella, 98–99

al-Qaeda, 25, 117–19

altruism, 52–53

American politics: credit and blame associated with, 25–29, 111–19; credit and blame at the time of the founding of, 22–25; 9/11, presidents, reputations and rankings of, 132–39. *See also* democracy

Appo, George, 89–90

Aramark Corporation, 43

Argentina, 55–57

Armin, 120–21, 148. *See also* Hermann Monument

Ashcroft, John, 116

Ashforth, Adam, 16–22

assignment of blame/credit: dangers of calling on public authorities to back up, 151; differences in blaming and crediting, 103–4; elements of, as judgments, 11–16; and implications for democracy, 150–51; and invoking a standard of justice, 6; and justice detection in legal proceedings, 35–42, 93–95 (*see also* justice detectors); the legal system and litigation as vehicle for, 33–34; psychological *vs.* social approach to, 6–8; as a social act, 3–5, 29–30 (*see also* social experiences/life); stories as vehicle for, 4–5, 20–22, 34, 39–42, 60 (*see also* stories); through truth and reconciliation commissions, 8–11; us-them boundaries and (*see* us-them boundaries); for wars, 127–32. *See also* blame; credit

awards. *See* honors

Axelrod, Robert, 108